# ECHOES
# FROM THE
# HOLOCAUST

# ECHOES FROM THE HOLOCAUST

## A Memoir

*Mira Ryczke Kimmelman*

The University of Tennessee Press •
Knoxville

**Library of Congress Cataloging-in-Publication Data**

Kimmelman, Mira Ryczke, 1923–   .
        Echoes from the Holocaust: a memoir / Mira Ryczke Kimmelman.—
1st ed.
            p.        cm.
        Includes index.
        ISBN 0-87049-968-8 (cl.: alk. pa.)
        ISBN 0-87049-956-4 (pbk.: alk. pa.)
1. Kimmelman, Mira Ryczke, 1923–   .
2. Jews—Poland—Gdansk—Biography.
3. Holocaust, Jewish (1939–1945)—Poland—Personal narratives.
4. Holocaust survivors—United States—Biography.
I. Title.
DS135.P63K557    1997
940.53'18'092—dc20
[B]                                          96-10013

*This book is dedicated to those I loved: my mother, brother, family, and friends. Their lives were brutally extinguished, but their memories live on.*

# CONTENTS

# ILLUSTRATIONS

*Maps*

# FOREWORD

On December 16, 1980, we gathered in formal attire in the Schatten Gallery of the Woodruff Library of Emory University to open the exhibit "Danzig 1939: Treasures of a Destroyed Community." The Judaica silver and the exquisite fabrics were stunningly displayed against the black background of a wintry night. The magnificence of the exhibit matched the splendor of the occasion. Among those present were a slim woman and her husband, survivors of another world. Mira Kimmelman and her husband, Max, had flown in to meet with the docents who were to lead tours of the exhibit and to be present for the gala opening. In those days, the only way to hear Mira's story was to listen to her tell it. Now she has written it down in this memoir. As I read it, I remembered her walking our docents through the exhibit, personalizing the objects so carefully displayed. Here was someone with whom we could connect the exhibit.

In retrospect, I wonder what is the true "exhibit"—the objects carefully sent by the community of Danzig and lovingly drawn together by The Jewish Museum for this traveling exhibit, or the life and story of Mira Kimmelman. The object exhibit has come and gone, and it was truly spectacular. Over twenty thousand people saw the exhibit in its few weeks at

Emory University, Charles Kuralt devoted a five-minute segment of his national program to it, and many wide-ranging changes resulted in the museum world of Emory and Atlanta. (See D. Blumenthal, "'Danzig 1939': An Exercise in Interfaith Understanding," *Emory Studies on the Holocaust,* ed. D. Blumenthal (Atlanta: Emory University, 1985), 136–44.) But the exhibit left, and those who came to Emory later do not even know it. Yet, the life of Mira Kimmelman has gone on. She has continued to live, to tell her story, and to reach some closure (as much as one can) with this piece of the past. This memoir tells her story, all of it: her beginnings in Danzig before the war, her life in the ghettoes of Poland, her experience of the kingdom of night, her life after her encounter with the world of death, and her pilgrimage back to the places of youth and terror late in her life.

Mira's story contains motifs that we who can only listen have heard before. She led a normal life in Danzig with family, friends, school, vacations, and Zionist youth groups. At that point, she and her brother wanted to leave (and could have left) for Palestine, but her parents were against it; they decided, fatefully, to stay together. When the situation worsened, they moved east to Warsaw and then to the smaller city of Tomaszow. Poverty, hunger, disease, and death followed them. They had to barter all their possessions for food; they had to burn furniture for warmth; they faced nazi (as a matter of principle, I do not capitalize this word) actions in the middle of the night; they underwent ghettoization. And yet Mira dared to take off her armband and travel to Warsaw to be examined in a secret school to continue her education, and she continued to lead youth groups. Eventually, she was separated suddenly from her mother, whom she never saw again, without even being able to say a proper goodbye.

As nazi pressure mounted, Mira was sent to the Blizyn Concentration Camp, to Auschwitz, and, after the forced march to Gleiwitz and the ride in the open flatcars to Germany memorialized so well in Elie Wiesel's *Night,* Mira wound up in Bergen Belsen. All the horrors of what the French call *le monde concentrationnaire* were present in Mira's life: rats the size of cats who came to the camp after having gorged themselves on the bodies of earlier prisoners who had been thrown into open ditches, the dog of the commandant who upon command tore live inmates to pieces, the "bread" made with sand and ground glass, the parents who led their children to the assembly point from which they did not return, and what Terrence des Pres in his book *The Survivor* calls "excremental attack," that is, the systematic depriving of the inmates of the ability to take care of their personal needs so that they had to defecate and urinate in their clothing. Imagine reaching out, touching the hand of your bedmate, finding it ice cold, and knowing that she has died during the night. No, I cannot even imagine that. And then there are the two sentences on thirst, a subject survivors mention and never talk about. (Worthy of research is Mira's assertion, made at several points, that women did better than men in the camps, on the death march, and then in the final agony before liberation.)

Reading such a memoir, we are upset, torn in our sympathy for the victim. Sometimes we have to put down the text because our reactions are so intense. The cruel evil is sometimes mixed with unbelievable good: the Jewish family which unhesitatingly hides a Polish doctor who, in turn, visits his patients later in the ghetto at great personal risk; the camp commandant who, though known as a sadist, protects "his" prisoners; the SS guard who offers the marchers a pair of military boots; the father who has a gold crown on his teeth pulled (without anesthetic) to be able to barter food for his child; the spontaneous sharing of food; and the simple sharing of women one with another. Goodness was rare but not absent, and that disorients those of us who have come to have a too-simple understanding of evil.

How does one survive? That is the question we ask, though the survivors do not. Mira, at different points in her memoir, ascribes her survival to the purpose of preserving a few family papers entrusted to her by her father; to a determination to outlive and outwit the nazis; to the sharing with other women prisoners; and to the need to remember what was happening so as to tell it later, to witness. In Mira's case, I think survival was due to fierce loyalty to her father and brother. This same fierce loyalty appears in her "afterlife" too—for her husband, for her children, and for the dead and the survivors. Mira's tending of the web of connectedness kept her alive, insofar as survival was at all within her power.

The last part of the book is devoted to several very touching recollections—of her brother, of her friend Eva, of her father, of her husband's "uncle," and then of her husband. These are beautifully written, and they perpetuate the memory of these fine people. So does the list of names of real people who died. So does the naming of her children, and her grandchildren. Yes, upon reflection, it is these eulogies, this list, and these resurrected names that are the true "exhibit" of what began in Danzig.

David R. Blumenthal
Jay and Leslie Cohen Professor
of Judaic Studies
Emory University

# ACKNOWLEDGMENTS

Writing this book was almost like giving birth to a baby. The process was long, obstacles many. Each step was painful; many tears were shed. Throughout this period I needed advice and support. Since this book can be viewed as a collection of stories, some repetition was unavoidable. A few stories are out of chronological order; this was done on purpose to establish emphasis. Without the assistance of many friends this memoir could not have been written. I am especially indebted to my editor and good friend, Professor June Adamson. For years she encouraged me to put my memories down on paper. She read, reread, and edited my manuscript. I owe her my deepest gratitude. The staunch support and earnest belief in my book of my learned friends Dr. John Bohstedt and Dr. Gerda Schmidt are greatly appreciated. They provided me with good counsel and guided me along the way. My profound thanks to Hanna Shapira for drafting the maps. I am beholden to Renee Bender, Jinx Bohstedt, Alexander Chervinsky, Martha Deaderick, Carol Minarick, Joel Swerlow, and many others who with their encouragement and friendship helped for this book to be born. The University of Tennessee Press has been most helpful and supportive; I cannot thank them enough. Last but not least: I want my children to know how much their patience, moral support, and most of all their love meant to me. This book was written for them, for their children and grandchildren.

# INTRODUCTION

Lawrence Langer, the foremost student of survivor testimony, has frequently said that everyone's Holocaust was different. The nature of each individual's experience might vary significantly depending upon which camp one was in and when one was there. Even within the same camp at the same time, the character of the experience varied significantly depending upon the section of the camp one was in or whom one encountered. Thus each survivor memoir tells a different story. Each account is an independent unit which contains in it a fragment of the complex phenomenon known as the Holocaust. A picture of that totality begins to emerge when the common threads of many memoirs, always mixed with unique and individual elements, are integrated. The more such integers we have, the clearer the picture that emerges. While it is historians such as Raul Hilberg who, through years of slow sifting of the mountain of documents in scores of archives, have reconstructed the framework of the Holocaust, it is the personal dimension of survivor memoirs that gives life to the historical evidence.

The prosecutors in Nuremberg in 1945 who were planning the first of the War Crimes trials knew that they could prove their cases from documentary evidence alone, without calling a single witness, thus avoiding the difficulties of memory—particularly the memories of often deeply traumatized individuals. However, they also knew that, if they wanted millions in Germany and around the world to be interested in the proceedings, they needed to introduce the individual human element. It is the combination of eyewitness testimony with the mountains of documentary evidence and the big-picture vision of the historian which has slowly sharpened our understanding of the Holocaust.

The videotaping of survivor accounts by the Yale documentary project, among others, offers hope that the invaluable source of direct-survivor presentation will be preserved even when there are no more survivors. However, interviews are often conditioned by the interviewer and, in their brevity, may create an impressionistic image shaped by the camera, resulting in a visual picture of the survivor vastly different from the testimony itself. Memoirs, on the other hand, embody years of reflection and careful presentation of experience. Thus, they give the reader a clearer sense of the nature of the events and their impact.

Mira Kimmelman is a survivor of Auschwitz, which she sees as representing absolute evil. Mrs. Kimmelman expresses the sentiment of many when she tells us that the world will never be the same after Auschwitz. Elie Wiesel in his own memoir says, "In truth, Auschwitz signifies not only the failure of two thousand years of Christian civilization, but also the defeat of the intellect that wants to find a Meaning—with a capital *M*—in history. What Auschwitz embodied has none. The executioner killed for nothing, the victim died for nothing." Yet Elie Wiesel and all Holocaust memoir writers feel the need to bear witness and do seek to find some sort of meaning in the horror. What Wiesel does caution us about is the rush to find hope and the triumph of the human spirit before we have really confronted the full terror and the reality of the distorted moral universe that was the world of the camps. The survivors must speak of that reality for the millions who cannot.

Mira Kimmelman grew up in Danzig, the Baltic seaport which between the world wars was a free city under League of Nations authority. Situated at the top of a corridor which was a wedge through German territory, Danzig gave the newly recreated Polish state access to the sea. It was an irritant which poisoned German-Polish relations and provided a powerful emotional issue for German right-wing nationalists. Danzig was a cosmopolitan and cultured city where Jews were mainly members of the middle class and were linguistically and culturally German. These Jews had, as Mira Kimmelman reminds us, unrealistic expectations about their future and could not comprehend the isolation, persecution, and life-threatening danger they would face when Nazism came to dominate Danzig. These expectations prevented many of Danzig's Jews, including the Ryczke family, from fleeing even though they possessed the means and the connections to emigrate, which most of their poorer and less-educated Eastern European brethren lacked. They refused to see the emerging violent hostility building on longstanding anti-Semitism as anything more than a temporary wave which would soon recede. In *The Diary of the Snail,* Germany's world-famous writer Günter Grass, a native of the Danzig area, contrasts the rising tide of Nazi racist politics in the city in 1938 with the stubborn reluctance of Danzig's Jews to believe that the city they loved and the culture they had enthusiastically embraced could harbor any real danger for them.

Mira Kimmelman describes her descent from the status of a "legally" equal citizen in Danzig to an exile and then a ghetto-dweller in Poland to a concentration-camp inmate. Her memoir adds to the literature which points out many of the conflicts and contradictions within Nazism itself. The conflict crucial to her life as an inmate centered on the question of slave labor. In a war period when labor was at a premium, those who wished to use Jews and other prisoners as slave laborers had to compete with those who saw Jews as destined only for the gas chambers. The Nazi slave-labor program was never a great success, and some of the factories built to utilize inmate labor in the area surrounding Auschwitz never produced anything as the pressure for victims for the gas chambers overwhelmed the need for laborers. As Mrs. Kimmelman tells us, even those factories that actually functioned were often places where overwork, starvation, disease, and frequent sadistic beatings took a fierce toll.

However, she also tells us that she and other inmates survived because some camps did employ slave laborers for periods of time and because certain German officials chose to keep some of these prisoners alive. While most inmates died after a few months of slave labor and most commandants sent their laborers to death camps at the first sign of disease or weakness, the confusion on the need for slave labor in factories resulted in some fortuitous exceptions. Mrs. Kimmelman testifies that S.S. Hauptführer Heller did not report a typhoid epidemic among laborers which would have sent them all to the gas chambers and that Commandant Taube of the labor camp Auschwitz-Hindenburg never allowed a prisoner to be killed or sent a weakened or sick prisoner back to a certain death during the five months that she worked at that facility. Mira Kimmelman's memoir describes camp situations where selections sent some to their deaths while others were sent to work camps. The situation described in this memoir contrasted sharply with the accounts of survivors such as Jankiel Wiernik, who was at Treblinka where virtually everyone was marked for immediate death.

Mrs. Kimmelman has wrestled with the question of how she survived years in the camps and the final "death march" from Auschwitz near the end of the war after those years of overwork, illness, and malnutrition. On the one hand, she identifies factors such as "the help of God, the support of friends, and kind deeds of those who shared food with us." On the other hand, she recognizes the role of luck in her survival, particularly as she relates her experience of Purim 1943. Many survivor memoirs talk of the role in survival of what Sonya Weitz calls "dumb luck." Each survivor has to cope with the knowledge that some of the most noble people they encountered died, as Primo Levi so eloquently reminded us, often because of their nobility. Some of the best died, some of the best survived, and often the difference between survival and death seems totally mysterious. In Mira Kimmelman's case, she and her father survived while her mother and brother died. Her father survived at one stage because a camp official called "Brillock," known for his cruelty and sadism, was fond of him.

Long-term concentration-camp survival, while always in part determined by luck, was also the result of personal strengths on the part of the individual prisoner. In the case of some Holocaust survivors such as Mira Kimmelman, a comment made during his prison years by Sean McStiofan, an IRA field commander, comes to mind in spite of the great differences in their circumstances. He said that whoever can endure the most, can suffer the most, will eventually triumph. Mira Kimmelman's total innocence and lack of any aggressive action against the German state or any individual was never in doubt, but her endurance and capacity to deal with acute suffering never faltered as well. Mrs. Kimmelman tells us that Hitler wanted to take away the humanity from his "enemies," particularly the Jews. Surrounded by death and brutality, ravaged by starvation and dysentery, enduring having her body brutally shaved by S.S. men, Mira Kimmelman succeeded in retaining her humanity.

A significant post-Holocaust part of Mira Kimmelman's book deals with a new life, a love, a family, and a new country. The United States, which had not opened its doors fully when it might have saved many more in the 1930s, proved a land of opportunity for Mira Kimmelman as for many other survivors in the period following the war. Although at the time it was easier for a Ukrainian or Lithuanian with a questionable war record to enter the United States than it was for many Holocaust survivors, Mira Kimmelman persevered. She took advantage of the new life the United States afforded her.

The Holocaust was primarily a tragedy for its victims—those who died and those who survived but bore its scars. However, the Holocaust was also a tragedy for the European civilization that spawned it. Certainly Germany and Central Europe as well as most of Eastern Europe became, as the Nazis dreamed it would, "judenrein." That process robbed Europe of a significant part of its history and of a creative, hard-working, and productive segment of its population. One of the less commented-on insights illuminated by survivor literature is the vital and positive part Jews played in cities like Danzig and countries such as Germany and Poland. These areas have suffered a loss from which they will not recover and of which German and Polish historians and writers have begun to show a growing awareness. The United States is a beneficiary of the refugee outpouring from Nazi Europe and the smaller stream of postwar survivors. Their lives and accomplishments have enriched our country, and their memoirs mingle now with the memory currents that contribute to what we are today.

Mira Kimmelman is a woman of great dignity and great heart, and her ability to see goodness as well as evil in the world and to give of herself to family and community is inspiring. Although she saw the worst, she managed somehow to retain some faith in the best. Unlike the survivor and writer Jean Amery, who permanently lost his trust in the world, Mira Kimmelman has succeeded in maintaining hope and rekindling a spark without ever losing the memory of what she saw and experienced. Hitler did indeed try to rob his "enemies" of their humanity. In Mira Kimmelman's case he failed.

Paul Bookbinder
University of Massachusetts, Boston

# TIMELINE

The following dates chronicle Mira Kimmelman's time in ghetto and concentration camps.

| | |
|---|---|
| Leaving Danzig | October 1939 |
| Warsaw | October 1939–February 1940 |
| Tomaszow-Mazowiecki | February 1940–May 1943 |
| Blizyn-Majdanek | May 1943–July 1944 |
| Auschwitz-Hindenburg | August 1944–January 18, 1945 |
| Evacuation | January 18–February 1945 |
| Bergen-Belsen | February–April 1945 |
| Liberation | April 15, 1945 |
| End of the War | May 8, 1945 |

# Chapter 1

# LIFE IN DANZIG

Sweet childhood memories linger for a long, long time. Such are the memories of my life in Danzig from earliest times until my world there ended with the outbreak of World War II.

Born in the seaside resort of Zoppot, a suburb of Danzig, on September 17, 1923, I vividly recall the beauty of the white beaches, the blue Baltic Sea, and the many walks my parents took me on. A nanny was hired to care for me. How I loved this gentle woman, Fräulein Medich. I even remember the fragrance of her clothes, always with the clean aroma of lavender. With her I explored the woods around Zoppot and admired the annual Blumenkorso, a parade of floats covered with the most beautiful flowers.

Then came the coldest winter in the history of Danzig—the winter of 1927. For the first time in centuries the Bay of Danzig was frozen solid. A thick sheet of ice reached as far as the town of Hel, which belonged to Poland. People walked across the bay as if it were land. We seldom had snow, but this winter brought an abundance of white. My parents took me sleigh riding for the first time. My mother too took part in guiding the sled, and with me in the back she ran into a pole. Nothing happened to me. I simply fell off and landed in the soft snow. But my mother's forehead was cut, and she had many bruises. This was my mother's last sleigh ride.

The birth of my brother, Benno, in January 1928 was an important event in my life in Zoppot. Until now my father commuted daily to his office on Frauengasse in Danzig. Commuting became harder for him because he was working longer hours. He was in the wholesale and export business of seeds and grain to the United States, Holland, and England. Our move from Zoppot took place at the end of March 1928, while Benno was a baby.

What a change this move was for me. Now we lived in the center of the city, on Brotbänkengasse, a stone's throw from the Mottlau River. Our huge apartment on the third floor had large rooms, one of which was transformed into my father's office. My brother and I shared an enormous bedroom. I recall riding my toy car with my name painted on the front in that room. The car was a birthday gift from my paternal grandparents. My brother, two by then, received a rocking horse.

The move meant no more daily excursions to the beautiful seaside. Now we explored the charm of the city of Danzig. On Sundays our family also took rides by boat to many places near the city.

Fräulein Medich left with us for Danzig, but not for long. She was engaged to a man who worked at the Langfuhr crematorium, and the couple planned to marry when she left us in 1930. My parents hired a housekeeper named Gertrude Jankowski. She quickly became the center of life for Benno and me. She introduced us to parts of Danzig we never knew. Excursions to the suburbs of Ohra, Oliwa, and Praust every May were highlights of the year. Long walks in the woods and near the water taught us about the nature around us. Gertrude was our teacher and friend. An orphan, she had a brother in Detroit who sent her packages with the nicest fabrics to make dresses, as well as cans with peaches and pineapple we never saw. Another of her brothers lived in Danzig and worked as a policemen. His name was Karl Jankowski. On her days off, Wednesdays and Sundays, Gertrude traveled to Meisterswalde, a small farm village to visit her foster family. She would bring us apples, pears, and plums from there when they were in season. But most of all we wanted to hear stories about her foster family and life on the farm.

By 1937 Nazi laws were getting quite strict in Danzig. One day Gertrude came to my parents and told them what her brother, Karl, had said: "You have to leave the Ryczke household. Soon the Nuremberg Laws will go into effect here and you will be punished if you remain with a Jewish family." My parents understood, and early in 1938 Gertrude left us.

We cried bitter tears. For almost eight years Gertrude had guided and taught us and was as close to us as if she were related. She had been an integral part of our family and knew all our secrets. All four of us loved her. She came to visit a few times. We were surprised to hear that she planned to marry the oldest son of her foster parents, Otto Schlicht. He was paralyzed and had to be in a wheelchair. Gertrude would take good care of him. I have wondered many times what happened to her and her husband. Where did they go after the Soviets took over Danzig in 1945? All that is left are fond childhood memories of her.

Ella Liedtke was among the people who influenced my life in Danzig. She was a socialist and an ardent anti-Nazi who worked for my father as a secretary and was quite outspoken about her political views. She had a talent for drawing and, whenever she had a free moment—my father's office being part of our apartment—I asked her to draw pictures of flowers, landscapes, and animals. I could watch her for hours. I learned from her too and drew pictures of my own. When my father moved his office away from our home to Milchkannengasse, Miss Liedtke went with him. In 1938 she left my father when we moved to Gdynia. She took a secretarial job with my father's friend there.

I met Ella Liedtke again after the war when she lived in the city of Passau after leaving Danzig. She remembered the time I spent watching her draw pictures. I lost contact with her after we left for the United States, but my father corresponded with her until her death.

When I was six and a half in 1930, I started public school. By 1934 the political situation in Danzig began to deteriorate with Hitler's rise to power. Although Danzig was a Free City, with a Senate and self-rule, it also had a high commissioner appointed by the League of Nations. A Swiss diplomat, he was trying to implement human rights for all, but members of the Senate were mostly Germans who joined the Nazi Party. Many street fights took place in the early 1930s, especially between the brown-shirts (Nazis) and the Social Democrats. Most of the time the Nazis won the fights. A strong Communist Party also existed in Danzig, and its members too were targeted by the Nazis.

While we lived on Brotbänkengasse, my father's younger brother, Heinrich, moved into our apartment. He was ten years younger than my father, and since he was born deaf, we had to learn to communicate with him using sign language and lip-reading. We loved him dearly.

The language used in Danzig was German; the culture was German. Only the railroad and part of the postal service were Polish. Both my parents had Polish citizenship, although my father was born and brought up in the Prussian part of Poland and attended German schools before World War I. My mother was born in Kalisz, which once was the part of Poland ruled by the Russians. She spoke fluent Russian and had many Russian-speaking friends in Danzig. Because this city and its surrounding area had the status of a Free City, many Jewish refugees from Russia came to live there after the Russian Revolution started. At one point Danzig and vicinity, with a population of 350,000, had 10,000 to 12,000 Jews.

In 1933 we moved to a larger apartment on Dominikswall #10. Also located on the third floor, it had eight rooms, two of which were my father's office. Benno and I now had separate rooms. After finishing three years of grade school, I was moved to the Victoria Schule, the German Gimnasium in Danzig. When Nazi laws were introduced in Danzig by 1935, the Jewish population began to shrink. First the "free professions," such as doctors, lawyers, public servants, and professors, lost their jobs. Dr. Hans Bing, our favorite doctor and a personal friend of my parents, left Danzig. Although married to a non-Jewish woman, he did not feel safe anymore. Other Jewish friends began seeking visas to move to other countries.

My first traumatic experience with Nazi rules was my expulsion from the German Gimnasium. Jewish students were not allowed to attend German schools, which was devastating for a twelve-year-old. My friends did not want to talk with me, my teachers ignored me. We, the Jewish students, felt completely isolated.

Jewish schools were being formed. A Jewish Gimnasium was started in the suburb of Langfuhr, but my parents decided that I should enter the private Polish Gimnasium, only a fifteen-minute walk from our apartment. Not knowing the Polish language, I had to be tutored for many months and then pass the entrance exams. I remember how bitterly I cried every night. Polish is a difficult language to learn at best. I was somewhat comforted by the fact that many of my friends were in a similar situation. In the fall of 1935 I entered the Polish Gimnasium. As anti-Semitism grew in the city, it was also reflected in the new school. By 1938 Jewish students in my class were forced to sit at desks separated from the Polish students. I had one close Polish girlfriend, Tula, who was told not to speak to me in school. None of this was pleasant.

To keep up the morale of the Jewish students, many Zionist and Revisionist Youth groups formed. All of us joined one of them. So did adults. Both of my parents were active in the Zionist movement.

While living in Danzig, both my brother and I took private Hebrew lessons. We had a scholarly teacher named Mr. Glueckmann, who instructed us in Bible, history, and Hebrew. But with the deteriorating situation for Jews in Danzig, in 1938 Mr. Glueckmann and his wife left for Paris where their son lived and where they hoped to be safe.

By now most of my parents' friends had secured visas and were leaving Danzig. Those of Polish nationality left for Poland. Others went to Holland, Belgium, England, France, and a few to the United States. Although both sets of my grandparents resided in Poland, my parents believed it was still safe to remain in Danzig. By the end of 1938 only about thirty-nine hundred Jews remained in Danzig and vicinity. Transports were going to Palestine and Shanghai. My music teacher, who came to Danzig from Hungary, left with her family for Manchuria.

Mira in her father's arms at eight months. Zoppot, May 1924.

Mira, age three. Zoppot, 1926.

Mira and her parents. Baby brother Benno is in the carriage. Zoppot, 1928.

Mira's first day of school, carrying the traditional cone filled with sweets. Danzig, April 1, 1930.

Mira's brother, Benno, age five. Zoppot, 1933.

Mira, age eleven. Orlowo, Poland, July 1934.

Mira's parents, Eugenia (Genia) and Moritz Ryczke. Gdynia, Poland, December 1938.

Mira Ryczke in Danzig, March 1939, before Hitler's army invaded the city on September 1.

In 1938 Jewish businessmen who still made their living in Danzig were constantly harassed by the tax inspectors. Trumped-up charges against Jews caused many of them to flee at night to avoid arrest. My father was warned by a German friend that an inspector would come to his office to examine his books. That evening my father left for the Polish city of Gdynia, only forty kilometers from Danzig. When the inspector came, the office clerks showed him the books. Everything was in order, but my father decided that for the time being we should leave Danzig. He rented an apartment in Gdynia on Swietojanska Street #66. We still kept our Danzig apartment and went back and forth for a few months. My brother, who was now also a student in the Polish Gimnasium, and I commuted daily to school in Danzig. We were with many friends and enjoyed the train rides, so for us this was fun.

While in Gdynia, I contacted a group of young Jewish chalutzim (pioneers) who were preparing themselves for life in Palestine. They wanted to learn fishery and settle near the Sea of Galilee. The fishing business in Gdynia was an excellent preparation with good schooling. I too wanted to leave for Palestine and spent many hours with this group of idealistic young people practicing Hebrew and learning all I could about life and culture in the land of Palestine.

By 1939 Hitler had conquered Austria and entered the Sudeten part of Bohemia and later occupied Czechoslovakia. Refugees from there were coming to Gdynia on their way to safe havens overseas. We housed many of them and learned the horrors they had endured. Yet my father was optimistic. He was so sure that there would be no war that we returned to our apartment in Danzig in the early summer of 1939. In the meantime, I applied for a certificate to go to Palestine to attend the agriculture school in Ben Shemen, without informing my parents of my plans. I did not want to upset them. In August 1939 I was notified that a "Shaliach," a messenger, would examine the applicants in Warsaw, and I was given a date to report there. Now I had no choice but to tell my parents about my plans.

My father was against my leaving the family, but I had an ally in my dear mother. She did not share my father's optimism and asked many times that we should leave Europe. Finally, she convinced my father that I should be allowed to go, and she went with me to Warsaw. The school accepted me, but I had to leave all my papers and my passport in Warsaw in order to receive the certificate and visa. The time was August 1939. One week after we returned to Danzig the war broke out.

My father's money was tied up in grain and seeds stored in granaries. Some of our jewelry was in the safety deposit boxes in Danzig and in Amsterdam. With the outbreak of war, all property, everything belonging to Jews, was confiscated. All we had were the valuables we kept in our home.

War broke out on September 1, 1939 at 4:45 A.M. We could hear the artillery shooting far away in the harbor where the Polish army defended the Westerplatte. My father went outside but soon returned. He was warned that Jews of Polish nationality would be arrested. On the second day we were ordered out of our apartment. All we could take with us were personal possessions. Each of us carried one suitcase. I was not very practical. Instead of putting in extra shoes and more clothing, my photo albums and stamp collections filled the suitcase. Thus we left our Danzig home, each carrying a suitcase and each hoping to return some day soon.

Most of the Jews were placed in apartments occupied by other Jews. We and a group of Polish citizens were taken to the oldest part of Danzig to an empty granary. Sleeping on a bare cement floor, with poor sanitary facilities, we soon learned that many of the Jewish men were caught in the streets and sent to the concentration camp of Stutthof not far from Danzig. This would have been my father's fate, had he not been with us in the granary.

From members of the Jewish community who brought us food we learned that Hitler would have his victorious entry into Danzig on September 19. The whole city was excited. Everyone except the Jews wanted to see the Fuehrer. For the few Jews still living in the city, this was a time of doom.

Nazis arrested Poles and Jews on the route Hitler would travel and sent them to Stutthof Concentration Camp where most of them perished. One of them was Bruno Chaim, my first boyfriend, who lived in Gdynia.

He was arrested early in September 1939, sent to Stutthof, and four months later his family was notified about his death, attributed to "a weak heart." He was twenty years old.

When hostilities against Poland ended and Warsaw capitulated, we, with some other Jewish citizens of Poland, were deported to Warsaw. Suitcases in hand, we walked to the Danzig railroad station and were ordered into freight cars. In my heart I said farewell to Danzig. The city of my childhood, the city I loved, where I had grown up and learned to cherish my Jewish tradition and my Zionist dreams, had expelled us. The Nazis wanted Danzig to be the first city to be Judenrein (free of Jews). The world I knew fell apart. My life felt shattered. Yet the fond and painful memories of my early childhood in Danzig are still with me. I try to recapture the good memories, the ones that helped me grow and mature.

# Chapter 2

# WARSAW

My parents, younger brother, and I had arrived in Warsaw from our home city of Danzig in mid-October 1939. The weather had already turned colder, and the room we occupied was extremely cold. With little fuel available, only the dining room was heated.

We had been given the room that belonged to my cousin Marysia, who married shortly before the war broke out. How well I remembered this room. Only two months earlier I had come here with my mother to finalize my exit visa for Palestine, then returned home to Danzig. Now this seemed so long ago, before our world collapsed.

The Warsaw I saw then did not exist now. Gone were the beautiful patrician buildings, destroyed by bombs. The wide boulevards lined with trees, elegant hotels, and coffee houses were in the past. What I saw now was a city in ruins and crowded with people sent here from other parts of Poland, many without a place to sleep. Jewish refugees sought shelter in destroyed buildings and cellars.

We too were uprooted, deprived of our possessions, uncertain of the future. Yet we felt fortunate to be able to stay with relatives. The small room on Nowolipki Street #19 became our temporary home. My father desperately looked for a larger place, knowing that we could not stay indefinitely with Aunt Gustava and Uncle David. But there was little hope of finding anything. In the meantime my mother caught a bad cold, which turned into pneumonia. She stayed in bed most of the time to keep warm. My relatives chopped wood from chairs and old tables to heat the one room. The rest of the apartment stayed biting cold. Life looked hopeless to us in this big city. We had to decide what to do.

While taking care of my sick mother, my thoughts turned to our time in Danzig when she told my brother and me stories about her youth. She was the second of three daughters and had two brothers as well, the oldest being Stasiek. Of the five, Henry was the youngest. My maternal grandparents owned a lace and embroidery factory in Kalisz, a city famous for its fancy lace, which was shipped to Russia to grace ladies' underwear and linens. When World War I broke out in August 1914, Kalisz was the first city conquered by the Germans. The conquering army burned the first city they entered, and Kalisz was almost completely destroyed. My grandparent's factory was entirely burned. But the house they lived in, not far from the factory, was still standing. Even so, they fled in the middle of the night.

My maternal grandparents loaded their children and a few personal possessions in a horse-drawn wagon and left for a nearby town. Because they didn't have room in the wagon for all the bedding they would need, my mother and her older brother, Stasiek, were sent back to fetch it from their home. My mother was only a seventeen-year-old girl at the time, but she was not afraid to return to the burning city. When the two came to their home, Stasiek went into the house and threw down pillows, comforters, and featherbeds from the window while my mother caught them and arranged them in the wagon. The work was done in a hurry, again in the middle of the night so no one would see them.

Although they reached my grandparents safely, my mother never forgot this experience. She often said to us: "I hope I never have to live through another war. Having experienced the loss of everything my parents had worked for, the city of my birth burned down, I hope I never have to see war

Left to right: Mira's cousin, Marysia Lachman; Mira's Aunt Gustava
Hammer Lachman; and cousin Michael Lachman. Warsaw, 1932.
Marysia, her baby and husband; her parents, Gustava and David
Lachman, all perished at Treblinka. Only Michael survived the war.

Mira's maternal
grandparents (left
to right) Sarah
Szmant Hammer
and Shlomo
Hammer, Kalisz,
Poland, 1930. Both
were killed in the
Warsaw ghetto.

again." After that she became frightened very easily. The courage she displayed as a young girl was gone.

A friend once asked me, "What was your mother like?" First and foremost, she was a lady. Composed, serene, calm, and quiet, although sometimes full of life, she had a soothing influence upon me. A volunteer as long
as I can remember, my mother was active in Zionist and philanthropic

causes. As for weaknesses, yes, my mother had two. She was a chain smoker, and she loved to gamble. The temptation was right where we lived in Zoppot. This seaside resort had a famous casino, which my mother frequented too often. She played for fun. Sometimes she won. Sometimes she lost. I remember one weekend she lost a considerable sum of money. This was her last time at the roulette table. I was very young, but I still remember that weekend. From then on cards became my mother's recreation. She became an excellent bridge player and spent three or four afternoons a week playing. Most of her friends were also her bridge companions. She enjoyed the game to the fullest.

As I looked at her now, sick in her sister's apartment, a refugee in wartorn Warsaw, all I wanted to do was to cheer her up, not easy under the circumstances we found ourselves. How long will we have enough jewelry to barter for food, I wondered?

My father, who was a perpetual optimist and would not believe that Germans could have bad intentions toward the Jews, was still hopeful. He remembered the Germans from before and during World War I. He worked with them and for them. How could they change so rapidly? My mother, on the other hand, was a realist. She had experienced the brutality as they entered Kalisz. She believed the worst. My mother urged that we leave Danzig, but my father resisted. My mother had persuaded my father that I should be allowed to leave for Palestine. As I grew she had become my closest friend. She taught me to be patient, to exercise self-restraint. I loved her deeply, but it was my father whom I idolized even after I saw how he misjudged the political situation, even after I realized that he kept us in Danzig when we were in a position to leave. I knew that he wanted us to stay together as a family, and believed that no harm would come to us as long as we, his children, were near him and our mother. For as long as I can recall, my father's role was always as our protector. And now, when we faced the dismal situation in Warsaw, it was my father who made the decision for us to leave. He still believed that by going to a smaller city we could make our lives more livable, and more comfortable and less worried. "We have to leave Warsaw. In a smaller town there will be a better chance for us to survive the war," my father had said as we sat in my aunt and uncle's small apartment where we had been staying. Unfortunately, it did not turn out that way.

My father left for Lodz to see his parents and his sister's family. As part of the German Reich, Lodz was renamed Litzmannstadt. In the meantime, my grandparents and other relatives had decided to leave Lodz when they learned a ghetto was being established. They moved to the city of Tomaszow, about seventy kilometers away. Tomaszow Mazowiecki, like Warsaw, was part of the General Government and had similar laws concerning Jews. Back in Warsaw, my father told us about his parents' decision to leave Lodz and began to plan for us to join them.

Things were changing for us too rapidly, however. By the end of November the Nazis ordered all Jews to wear the white armband with the blue Star of David on their outer clothing. Also, a curfew went into effect for the Jews. We were forbidden to leave our living quarters from the time it got dark in the evening until it was light in the morning. Jews were also forbidden to use any public transportation—trains, buses, or trams.

Jewish men were afraid to venture outside even in daylight, for Germans were catching men to clear the city's ruins, to clean the rubble from Warsaw's streets, and to shovel snow. Nazis were also beating and shooting Jews. With my mother ill, I was the only one to go outside to get food for the things I could barter. At age sixteen I had to learn fast how to avoid being caught.

I soon learned that some of my school friends from Danzig had also found refuge in Warsaw. Two of them were Janka and Lusia Krakowska. They had escaped to Warsaw in September, while their parents had managed to leave for England before the outbreak of war. Now they seemed trapped in Warsaw. Later however, their parents paid someone to smuggle the two sisters out of Poland. Traveling through Austria and Hungary, they were reunited with their parents in England in the summer of 1940.

By early February 1940 my mother's health had improved and my father made plans for our escape from Warsaw. It would not be easy. To travel by train we would have to remove our armbands. And we had to pretend we were strangers from each other as we walked to the train—a safety measure.

The weather was bitter cold on the morning we left Warsaw. Dressed in layers of clothing to keep warm, we carried only small bags with our belongings. Venturing into the below-zero winter day, the four of us walked separately to the train station. My parents instructed my brother and me to walk on, not to look back should the Nazis stop one of us. Families were punished as a unit. We had to pretend that we were strangers.

At the crowded station we had to stand on the platform for hours waiting for a train that would take us to Tomaszow. Our hands and feet were numb from the cold. Only one train came by, but it was already overcrowded and we could not get on. Because it was getting dark, we were forced to return to our relative's home. All of us had frostbitten fingers and toes. Yet, after a night's sleep, my parents were determined to try to leave again. On the second day we succeeded in boarding a train going to Koluszki. From there we would have to transfer to another train destined for Tomaszow.

From a distance I could see my brother, father, and mother getting on the train, each one boarding a different car, as I did. At the first stop, the door of the car I was in was opened by Nazi officers. "Alle Juden raus" (All Jews out), they shouted. I sat motionless. My heart was beating so hard, I hoped the people sitting next to me did not hear it. Pretending to read a book, I did not move.

The realization that I had to make believe that I was not Jewish hit me sharply. "Would the Nazis ask for my papers?" I wondered, knowing that I carried an old registration document and on it was my religion. The fact that I, a Jew, traveled by train without my armband would have been enough for the Nazis to take me off the train and have me shot. But God was watching over me. The Nazis looked at each passenger, closed the door, and left.

My outward calm saved me. If I wanted to live, outwitting the Nazis was a necessity. I first learned this lesson during our escape from Warsaw.

# Chapter 3

# NEXT STOP:
# TOMASZOW MAZOWIECKI

I never heard the name "Tomaszow" until we arrived there in February 1940. We found a fairly young city compared to Poland's major cities, only about a hundred years old. It had a population of about 100,000, 10 percent being Jews. The city was especially well known for its many textile mills that produced excellent wool yarn spun and dyed to make fabric. Most of the specialists in Tomaszow's textile mills were of German origin or were ethnic Germans, but most of the owners were Jews.

My paternal grandparents, along with my father's only sister, Rose, her husband and two daughters, had rented a three-room apartment after they arrived here from Lodz. One of these rooms became our new home. The kitchen had to be shared with other tenants, which was not always convenient. But at least here we had enough fuel to heat the apartment, and food was also much easier to obtain than in Warsaw.

We were glad to be here, to be close to our family and in a city that was not demolished by bombs. But there were surprises in store. No sooner did we settle when the Gestapo (the secret police) requisitioned the whole building we lived in for their headquarters. Again we had to take our belongings and find a place to live. My grandparents and Aunt Rose and her family found a small place nearby, and we moved to a room on Warszawska Street #5.

My father was still optimistic. He believed that by spring the war would be over. "This war cannot last long. Poland is in Hitler's hands. Soon there will be peace," he said in March 1940. We wanted to believe him, but a few weeks later the news of Hitler's invasion of Denmark and Norway reached us. Now we all knew that this war would not end soon.

The Jews of Tomaszow lived throughout the city. Now we had to obey the laws of curfew. Jews were not allowed to walk outside when it was dark, and we had to wear the white armbands with their blue Star of David on our right arms, just as we had in Warsaw. At first we felt like strangers; we were refugees. Except for our grandparents, Aunt Rose, her husband, Marcus Przedecki, and my two cousins, Halina and Gina, we had few friends. Unable to go out in the evenings, we made friends with people living in the same house, and with neighbors on the street. How lucky I was that one floor above us lived the Weiskopf family, whose daughter, Sala, was my age. We became close friends.

Sala's parents were respected citizens of Tomaszow since both were dentists. The house they lived in before moving to Warszawska Street was hit by a bomb and burned. Sala had an older brother, Zygmunt, who was a medical student at Montpelier in 1939. But when he came home for the summer vacation, he could not return to France. The youngest daughter, Zosia, was my brother's age.

As spring turned into summer, living conditions grew steadily worse. Constant raids into Jewish homes were carried out by the SS (the Nazi elite in charge of all concentration camps) or the Gestapo. They ransacked everything and took whatever was of value. We had quite a few such raids. Fortunately my father hid our few valuables so well that the Gestapo never found anything. And these hidden pieces of jewelry became our only hope to obtain more food. Nobody wanted to sell foodstuffs for money except for dollars, pounds sterling, or gold. Jews were issued food stamps meant to last a month, but in one week they were gone and again we were hungry. Little by little, rings, watches, earrings, and gold coins were traded for bread, potatoes, and sugar. My brother was growing fast and needed more food than the rest of us. Only the black market provided additional food for the Jews of Tomaszow.

As more and more Jewish refugees arrived in the city, the Jewish Council organized soup kitchens for them. My Aunt Rose was hired as supervisor in one of these kitchens and took her two daughters and me to help out as waitresses. We did not get money for our work but were paid with a bowl of soup. This additional food sustained me throughout the summer and autumn of 1940. I was also allowed to take home some leftovers, a welcome treat for my family.

As I walked home from the soup kitchen, dead tired from being on my feet for twelve hours, I would think back to my carefree life in Danzig. A year ago I was a happy teenager, a student in the Polish Gimnasium. Now I was working for a bowl of soup. I did not feel anger or shame, but a terrible sadness. I was willing to work as hard as possible to help my family with additional food, if only we could be together, if only things would not get worse.

My mother was unable to do the chores in our small room. They were left for my brother and me. She did the cooking in the kitchen shared with other tenants, little though there was to cook. When we had bread and boiled potatoes, we were quite happy.

The evenings were long. We did find some books so that my brother and I could go on with our education. My father tested us after we finished with a subject. We longed to be able to go to school, but it was forbidden for Jews. The same was true for praying, but almost every house had secret rooms for prayer, which was important to those who were truly religious and felt the need to pray. A few months later secret schools began to be organized.

With autumn approaching, there were many arrests of Poles. The Gestapo was searching for Polish doctors, lawyers, teachers, and past army officers. Rumors flew that they were being sent to Oswiecim, the Polish name for Auschwitz, near Cracow.

A Polish doctor and his wife lived in the next house to us, on

Mira's paternal grandfather,
Ephraim Ryczke. Danzig,
1931. He was killed at
Treblinka, November 1942.

Mira's paternal grandmother, Esther
Jakubowski Ryczke. Danzig, 1934.
She was killed at Treblinka,
November 1942.

Left to right: Mira's uncle, Marcus Przedecki; his daughters, Gina and Halina, and
Mira's aunt, Rose Ryczke Przedecka, 1928. All were killed during the Holocaust.

Warszawska #7. He was Dr. Stefan Giebocki and had come with his wife,
Maria, to Tomaszow from Bydgoszcz. They too were refugees. We became
good friends, and I even tutored Dr. Giebocki in German.

One early morning in October 1940, we heard a knock at our door. We
couldn't imagine who it might be. Maria Giebocka stood there. In a quiet
voice she told us that the Gestapo was on our street searching for Polish
doctors. "Could my husband hide in your room until things get normal
again?" she asked. Without hesitation my parents told her that Dr. Giebocki
was welcome to stay with us for as long as he had to. My parents knew the
danger of harboring a Polish doctor, yet it did not matter. He was a friend
who needed our help.

Dr. Giebocki came over dressed in women's clothing so that nobody
would recognize him. For three days and nights he stayed in our small room,

sleeping on my cot, while I shared my mother's bed. Nobody in the house could know that we were hiding him, so we had to keep very quiet. Our windows faced Warszawska Street. We could see the columns of heavily guarded Poles being marched to the railroad station by the Gestapo. Their destination was Oswiecim, a place nobody knew anything about. Nor could anyone guess their fate.

After three days Maria Giebocka came to take her husband home. The Gestapo did visit her to ask for her husband. She told them that he had to leave for Warsaw to visit his sick mother. Dr. Giebocki never forgot what my parents did for him. When months later we were forced to move to the ghetto and my mother became ill, he visited her as often as she needed his help. He too risked his freedom for us, because it was forbidden for Poles to treat Jews, especially to enter the ghetto to do so. Stefan Giebocki was a true friend.

Sadly, we learned the fate of Dr. Giebocki after the war. While searching for my brother, my father stopped in Tomaszow. He tried to look up the doctor, the only friend we had outside of the ghetto. Dr. Giebocki was dead. My father was told that it was suspected that Dr. Giebocki had been poisoned. Rumors had it that it was by his wife. He was a handsome man, and his wife was known to be very jealous.

*Chapter 4*

# TOMASZOW GHETTO

## *Trials and Tribulations*

The announcement about the creation of a ghetto in Tomaszow Mazowiecki came as no surprise to us. Since February 1940 when we arrived in this city, we knew that in many cities ghettos had been created and that it would probably happen here. But we could not realize what poor conditions of life awaited us.

The poorest and most dilapidated part of Tomaszow, where until now many Polish families lived, had been designated to become the ghetto. A church stood on Wiecznosc Street, but it did not prevent the street from becoming part of the newly created Jewish ghetto.

The order to move was announced the beginning of December 1940, giving us just a few weeks to find a place to live. When the Polish population moved out of their houses, Jews were moved in. Until now most of the Tomaszow Jews lived in apartments. Now they had to squeeze into one room, in some cases two and three families to occupy one room. The Jewish Council, made up of twelve prominent Jews selected by Nazi officials to administer ghetto life, was in charge of assigning living quarters. My fam-

ily was assigned to one room on Zgorzelicka Street #37. Our new "home"—
one small room—was our bedroom, living room, kitchen, and bathroom.
Although this house had indoor plumbing, we were not allowed to use the
kitchen or the bathroom. My brother and I had to bring water from the pump
in the yard. And my poor mother, whose health was not good, had to use the
outhouse even in the coldest weather. Yes, we were refugees, and as such,
even we became second-class citizens in the ghetto.

The house where we lived was the last one on the street near the ghetto
gate. Here we became virtual prisoners, unable to leave the ghetto unless we
had a special permit. And permits were given only to those Jews who were
employed outside the ghetto. Ration cards for bread, sugar, marmalade, or a
little margarine were issued for the whole month but barely sustained us for
a week. The alternative to starvation was bartering valuables or clothing.
Item by item, my parents parted with the few possessions we brought with
us from Danzig. I tried to "earn" extra bread by taking in clothing to be
washed and ironed. Learning English was becoming popular, so I was paid
with bread to tutor young children in the language.

Even before the ghetto was created, illegal schools for Jewish children
were flourishing—if, indeed, they could be called "schools." But in attics,
cellars, or private rooms children were being taught by Jewish teachers who
lived in the city. From the very beginning of the war, Germans not only prohibited the teaching of Jewish children but closed the schools as soon as they
entered a city. All assemblies by Jews were strictly forbidden: schooling,
worshipping, any congregating. Death was the punishment for those who
were caught disobeying. Yet, despite the severe prohibitions, Jewish children continued their education, and Jews in the ghetto continued to pray in
secret.

Because I was only one year from matriculating from what would be
called the high-school level in the United States, my parents insisted that I
continue my schooling in secrecy. Naturally they had to pay for it, but my
education was important to them and to me. We still believed that the war
would not last very long, and eventually I would be able to continue my
studies at a university. So I attended the illegal school as soon as we arrived

in Tomaszow and finished while we were in the ghetto. To take the matricu-
lation exams we had to travel to Warsaw. Again the problem of traveling
became an issue. My father insisted on accompanying me to Warsaw. This
time we traveled by bus, but removed our armbands to avoid recognition as
Jews. The risk was great. If caught we would have been imprisoned or even
shot.

We traveled to Warsaw early in May 1941. I had to report to a secret
address where professors from prewar gimnasiums were administering the
tests. I had to pass two kinds of exams, written and oral, which I did.

While I was occupied with the exams, my father took the time to visit
old friends from Danzig who were now living in Warsaw. From them he
found out that for money a person could obtain fake entry visas to South
American countries. With such a visa, the Gestapo would allow people to
leave Poland. The only item of value my father had with him was his gold
watch. Without thinking twice, he sold it to pay for four entry visas to Uru-
guay for our family. The prospect of prolonged life in the ghetto seemed
impossible, and the thought of escaping this depressing existence brought
new hope into our lives.

We were told that it would take three weeks for the visas to be
ready, so we returned to Tomaszow to inform my mother and brother of
our new plans for the future. My mother was euphoric. To have a chance
to leave this horrible ghetto life, to leave Poland and start anew in South
America, seemed too good to be true. She began to alter clothing and to
prepare for our departure.

Three weeks went by. My father went back to Warsaw hoping to return with our visas. When he came back a few days later, his face showed
the terrible blow he had suffered. The people who were forging visas had
been caught; the money he paid them was gone. But worst of all, our hopes
to leave Poland were shattered. We were caught in the net with no escape.

In the meantime I had outgrown not only my clothing but even my
shoes. We had no money to buy new shoes. Both of my big toes became so
infected that I could barely walk. My father cut out the leather on my shoes;
otherwise I would not be able to go outside. Somehow we learned that a

famous surgeon from the city of Lodz worked in the ghetto. Again some of our valuables had to be sold to pay for the surgery. The moment Dr. Mortkowicz saw my toes, he said both nails had to be removed. Because the pain was so excruciating and there was no anesthetic available, only one nail at a time could be removed. For the next few days I was in pain, and there was nothing available to ease it. The second nail was removed one week later.

Suddenly it occurred to my mother that she had heard the name Mortkowicz before; it was the name of our tailor in Danzig. She asked whether the doctor had relatives in Danzig before the war. He said, "Yes, I had a brother there—he was an excellent tailor. He could sew the nicest clothes. I am excellent in cutting," he added, meaning in surgery. So, by chance a brother of our tailor from the "good old days" in Danzig operated on me in the Tomaszow ghetto.

Part of my ghetto life was filled with work for the Zionist cause. From my early childhood in Danzig I belonged to the Zionist Youth movement. While in Warsaw I sought out the Hashomer Hatzair organization, and from them I had names of people who were active in Tomaszow. As soon as we settled in the city, I contacted the leader of the local Zionist Youth group, David Goldman. He was the son of an older couple who owned a restaurant. David's Yiddish nickname was "Dovid Lacher" (meaning "David who laughs"). He had the whitest teeth, and when he smiled all a person could see were his beautiful teeth. David entrusted me with leading small groups of Jewish youth. We met in secrecy every Saturday afternoon in cellars or attics. Such meetings were strictly prohibited even before the ghetto was created. Yet they were as essential for keeping up the morale of the young people as were the secret schools. They provided an escape from the bleak and hopeless realities of ghetto life and gave us hope.

Heated discussions about Jewish history, the hope for a Jewish home-land in Palestine, lessons in Zionist history, and the singing of Hebrew songs kept up our morale and gave purpose to the hopeless situation we had to face. I had never mentioned these Saturday meetings to my parents. Only my brother knew about them. Saturday afternoons were devoted to visits to my grandparents and other relatives. I did visit my relatives but never stayed as long as my parents expected me to. Instead, I devoted the rest of the afternoons to the secret meetings of the Zionist Youth group.

From time to time those of us in the group received pamphlets and news from other cities about their work in the Zionist movement. These materials were smuggled into the ghetto by runners. Most of them were young girls with Aryan looks—that is, blonde hair and blue eyes. These budding women risked their lives to bring such literature into the ghetto. The literature had to be well hidden, and after it was read at meetings, destroyed. One time I took some leaflets home to be used the following Saturday. Without my parent's knowledge, I hid them on the bottom of one of the chests of drawers. To my dismay, a few days later after curfew, we were surprised by a visit from two German soldiers. Because of the proximity of our house to the ghetto gate, we had quite a few such "visits." The soldiers were looking for money, valuables, jewelry. After they ransacked our room and did not find anything of value, they were ready to leave. Then they noticed the chest.

I was petrified and stood as if paralyzed while the soldiers opened drawer after drawer. "Dear God—please stop them. Do not let them find the illegal pamphlets," I prayed silently. Impatient and angry after throwing the contents of the first two drawers on the floor and not finding anything of value, they stopped without opening the last drawer, where the flyers were hidden. They left our room, loudly cursing the Jews.

The whole time of the search my parents were unaware of the danger I had exposed them to. Never again did I bring home anything that could jeopardize the lives of my family.

*Chapter 5*

# BLOODY APRIL 1942

Loud banging at the gate woke us in the middle of the night. When the gate was opened, we could hear heavy steps coming toward our door. Next came the kicking of the door. In the pitch dark, we did not dare turn on the lights. We heard shouts in German and women crying. The noises came from the apartment next to ours. Our walls joined and we could hear everything.

"Schnell, schnell—raus mit dir!" (Quick, Quick—get out!) The door slammed, and a few minutes later a single shot pierced the air.

No one was at our door, but we waited in darkness, paralyzed by fear. My mother and I shared the bed, and both of us were covered with cold sweat. "Had the Germans come for all the Jewish men? Would they return to take my father too?" we asked each other. We could not sleep. The rest of the night was spent in horror as we listened to sporadic shooting. With a nighttime curfew in the Tomaszow ghetto of Poland, we dared not leave our room until daylight.

As soon as it was light, my father went outside to learn what had happened during the night. Soon he returned, but white as a sheet. "Our neighbor has been shot. His body is in the gutter in front of the house," he re-

Left to right: Eva Kolska and Mira Ryczke, best friends in the Tomaszow-
Mazowiecki ghetto, 1942.

ported. "Why our neighbor? What did he do to be killed?" we wondered aloud.

As ghetto occupants stirred, others went into the streets too. News spread quickly. The victims of the Gestapo shootings were some of the Judenrat (Jews appointed by the Gestapo to carry out the administration of the ghetto), Jewish ghetto police, lawyers, doctors, former officers in the Polish army, and Jewish activists. Obviously the Nazis had prepared a list from which to choose victims. For example, one woman, the wife of the Jewish police chief, was also a victim of this massacre. She was shot down as she ran after her husband, one of the victims.

Tomaszow ghetto became one huge house of mourning. With many family members and friends dead, we were in total shock. As the warm April day wore on, the bodies of the victims were put on a cart to be taken to the Jewish cemetery outside the ghetto. Thousands of us accompanied the bodies to the ghetto gate to pay our respects and bid last farewell to friends and relatives. I walked in this sad procession with the two sons of the murdered lawyer. Their mother had died of typhoid only a few months before. Now they were orphans. These two young men, nineteen and twenty years old, were my friends. My parents and I walked with them, all crying bitterly. No words of comfort could ease their pain.

The next night was a repetition of the previous one. Again shots were heard throughout the night. This time our building was not visited, however. In the morning, my friend Eva and I ventured into the streets to learn who the latest victims were. I was horrified to see that among the murdered were the two sons of the lawyer who had been killed the night before—my friends. They were the youngest victims of the April killings in the ghetto. Yet only twenty-four hours before I walked with them behind the cart carrying their father's body. Now many of us walked behind the cart carrying their bodies to mourn their deaths.

Cries and laments were heard throughout the ghetto. The Jews of the ghetto were panic stricken, completely terrorized. We were afraid to sleep in our apartments, not knowing who the next victims might be. But, for the next few days and nights, all was quiet. Then came an order for all members of the remaining Judenrat to report to their office.

My father and I returned one day from a visit to my grandparents who lived nearby in the ghetto. As we walked down Stolarska Street, we saw a group of Gestapo in front of the Judenrat headquarters. My father turned his head to look at them, then literally cried out to me, "Don't turn around!" That moment two shots were fired behind us. My father did not want me to see the execution of members of the Judenrat.

We ran home as quickly as we could. My father said he had to warn Mr. Fischman, a friend who was a Judenrat member. Mr. Fischman was leaving his home to report to his office, so we barely caught him. "Do not go! The Nazis are killing the Judenrat!" my father said urgently, explaining what we had just witnessed. Mr. Fischman was a well-known textile industrialist with many contacts among the Poles of the city. Having listened to my father's warning, the Fischmans contacted Polish friends who helped them escape from the ghetto. They were kept hidden throughout the war years, survived, and moved to Israel.

The killings, however, continued for three April nights. The ghetto never recovered from the shock of the murders. We lost our leaders, our role models, some of our best people.

# Chapter 6

# THE WATCH

## *Liquidation of the Ghetto*

First came the shrilling shout: "Du verfluchtes Schwein" [you damned swine]! Suddenly I felt a cutting pain on my back, my shoulders, my head. The SS officer caught me as I ran down the stairs of the factory where the SS had taken us. It was October 31, 1942, the day when the liquidation of the Polish Tomaszow Mazowiecki ghetto began.

A few hundred Jews, mostly young men and women, were taken out of the marching columns as the others from our ghetto walked to the railroad station. We were told we were all being sent "east" to work. The true destination was Treblinka, the death camp, but at that time we did not know the truth about Treblinka. We had heard of other ghettos being "liquidated," a euphemism really meaning death. The Germans called it "Aussiedlung," which meant resettlement. Those who lived in the ghetto and worked for the Germans were assured that they and their families would remain in ghettos, however. The families of the Judenrat and Jewish ghetto police were told the same thing. Everyone frantically tried to find work in order to protect their families. Quick marriages were performed for people who had jobs and wanted to try to protect their loved ones.

My father and brother worked outside the ghetto for the Organization Todt (OT), a group that had a fleet of trucks to serve the Germans by moving supplies to the soldiers at the front. I had a job from May until July 1942 at the Heereswaescherei Schultz (army laundry), where blood-soaked uniforms from the eastern front were washed and repaired. But in July the laundry had closed and I was without a job. My mother and I stayed in the ghetto hoping that my father's job would enable us to remain where we were. A few days before this fateful day the families of all slave workers for the OT were taken to a safe place, an empty factory on Stolarska Street. Everyone envied us. They thought we were safe.

On the night of October 30, the ghetto was surrounded by SS soldiers and by Ukrainian SS guards. Only those working for the Germans were permitted to leave. Early the next morning all the men who worked for the OT left for work. Only the women and children remained in the empty factory.

Then, about 8 A.M., we heard the dreaded loud knocking at the door, which someone opened to the SS. They ordered everyone to assemble outside in ten minutes. "Wear your heavy working shoes, warm clothing, and carry all your valuables. You may need them," we were ordered.

Upstairs my mother and I dressed hurriedly in layers of clothing, packed extra warm garments into our rucksack and ran downstairs. In the rush I left my wristwatch, a thirteenth-birthday gift from my parents, forgotten as we were confronted by the brutality of the SS. We were marched five in a row down Stolarska Street toward the railroad station. From every corner, every street, Jews were marching; old ones, young ones, mothers with babies, children holding onto parents.

We marched in absolute quiet. Now and then a shot was heard, but we were too scared to look back. As we walked we saw an SS officer in front of a small white Catholic church surrounded by a graveyard pointing to people and pulling them out. As we got near him he pointed to me, ordering me to step out. It happened so quickly I had no time to turn to my mother, no time to say goodbye. She walked on with the column, and I never saw her again.

I must have been taken from the column because of my youth and because of my effort to look strong and braver than I really was.

Time passed slowly, as we, the selected young Jews, stood for hours in the churchyard. The day was exceptionally warm, the sun was shining, yet this was the darkest day in my life. At evening we were taken back to the empty factory on Stolarsta Street where my family and I had spent the previous night together. The SS ordered us to stay downstairs. Then I remembered the watch I had left upstairs. I thought, "I have to get upstairs and retrieve my watch." I found the chrome-plated Optima and hid it in my clothing. Then came the encounter with the SS officer, who caught me on my way downstairs. Why did I dare risk my life for a watch? An inner voice told me to get it.

Hurting from the whipping, sore from the brutal blows, I could not stop thinking of my family. My mother, grandparents, aunts, uncles, cousins were gone. Only my father and brother remained. I was so relieved to see them return when the OT workers were escorted back to the factory. Sitting on the cement floor of the factory, we grieved for our dear ones. Not knowing their fate, everyone hoped they had been sent to work. A few hours passed until the OT workers, including my father and brother, were ordered to leave the building where we were so they could sleep at their workplace. I felt lost and alone.

Suddenly the front door opened. A drunken Ukrainian SS guard entered. Rifle in hand, he grabbed the kind and gentle Jewish ghetto "Ordnungsdienst" (policeman), a friend of mine named Mietek Hendeles. He and his younger brother came to Tomaszow from Lodz. A decent, gentle person, Mietek took the job as a policeman to protect his family. The Ukrainian shouted in his drunken voice: "Give me a tchasoy [watch] or I shoot him," as he grabbed Mietek, but pointed his rifle at us. Not a sound could be heard. I reached for my watch, and handed it to the Ukrainian, who released Mietek and left the factory, satisfied. Now I knew why I ran upstairs to get my watch. The watch my parents gave me in Danzig in 1936 saved the life of a friend, the life of a kind person.

# Chapter 7

# PURIM 1943

Feeling chilled and achy, I got up to face another day of forced labor. The winter of 1943 was cold and wet, and the rooms we lived in were unheated. We, the remaining Jews of the ghetto of Tomaszow, had been herded into a smaller ghetto called "the Block," actually a block of houses, which were part of the former large ghetto. Here I lived with my father, brother, and uncle, the remnants of our family of eighteen.

At the time of the ghetto liquidation, almost sixteen thousand Jews lived here. In the smaller ghetto, we were just over six hundred, all that remained of the Jews of Tomaszow. We were the lucky ones who were still alive.

Like shipwrecked people clinging to a board, we clung to family members and friends who were spared the "resettlement east"—death at Treblinka. Left behind to clean the ghetto of the belongings of our dear ones, I was assigned at first to sort clothing and pack everything usable into crates destined for Germany.

My second job was in a newly created slipper factory where slippers were made for German soldiers out of unsuitable and torn drapes, rugs, and blankets that once belonged to the residents of the ghetto. While I worked with my uncle in the Dietz slipper factory, my father and brother worked for the Organization Todt (OT), a company incorporated into the army that served as a depot and shipped food and clothing to the German front.

A few families with children still lived in the "Block." One day the Nazis announced that there would be an exchange between German residents of Palestine and Jews from the Polish ghettos. A small number of families signed up. A few members of the Jewish intelligentsia were added to this group, and they were taken by trucks to the train station. Many who stayed behind envied them, but some were skeptical. Only a few days later we learned that the train they were on did not go west and then to Palestine but east to Treblinka.

Conditions in the Block became harsher, with random shootings occurring almost daily. My father asked his boss, Mr. Feldhege, if it would be possible for me to be transferred to the OT sewing division to put me closer to his place of work. The petition was granted. I became a seamstress, along with more than twenty other women. We worked repairing and sewing linens, gowns, and bandages for German hospitals.

On a dreary, cold, and damp day in March, I began to feel so ill that my work lagged behind. I could barely see. My head and throat ached. Unable to continue my sewing assignment, I reported sick to the German overseer and was escorted back to the Block by a Jewish policeman. He was ordered to take me to the makeshift hospital.

The so-called hospital was a small house with three rooms and a kitchen on the ground floor. One room was designated as a dispensary and operating room. A famous surgeon named Mortkowicz was the only doctor left in the Block. From Lodz, he and his ten-year-old daughter and a nurse lived in the hospital's upstairs. Of the two remaining rooms on the ground floor, one was for male patients and the other for females.

Dr. Mortkowicz examined me and diagnosed strep throat. My fever was climbing, and he ordered me to stay in the hospital three days. All I could do was rest and sleep; there was no medication except a few aspirin. I thought about what a strange coincidence this was. Here I was being treated by Dr. Morkowicz, the brother of our tailor in Danzig. The tailor made suits for our family before the war. On the second day I felt so much better that I decided against the doctor's wishes to return to work. I stayed in the hospital two days instead of the three the doctor ordered.

I shall never forget the day when I returned to work. It was Purim (March 21, 1943). Happy to join my father and brother, I went gladly back to my sewing machine. We had just stopped for lunch when all Jewish workers were told to assemble immediately in front of the buildings we worked in. Told to return right away to the Block, we entered the smaller ghetto escorted by the Jewish police. Because this was unusual, we felt uneasy. When all workers were back in the Block, a curfew was declared. We were ordered to stay in our rooms. Anyone leaving the living quarters would be shot, we were told.

My brother, uncle, and I complied. Only my father was missing. While the order to return to the Block was given, he was outside the city driving an OT truck. By the time the curfew was lifted, it was almost dark. My father was allowed to enter the Block and return to us. He was anxious to know the reason for our early return from work, since he knew nothing of the curfew.

The horrible truth and news of this day's happenings spread like wildfire once the curfew was lifted. The SS had surrounded our makeshift hospital, taken Dr. Mortkowicz, with his only daughter, the nurse, and all the patients who were in the hospital at the time. Then they took the rest of the intelligentsia. All were driven by truck to the Jewish cemetery. Open graves had been prepared ahead of time. The victims were ordered to undress, then lined up in front of the graves and murdered by machine-gun fire.

Had I stayed one more day in the hospital as the doctor ordered, I, too, would have been among the unfortunate victims on this fateful Purim day.

*Chapter 8*

# LIFE AND DEATH AT BLIZYN-MAJDANEK

*Typhoid Epidemic*

My father, brother, uncle, and I traveled by cattle car from the Tomaszow ghetto to the Blizyn Concentration Camp in May 1943. Located between the cities of Radom and Lublin, this camp became part of the notorious Majdanek Concentration Camp by the end of 1943.

Although I was separated from my dear ones and sent to the women's part of Blizyn, I could see my father and brother and uncle after the evening roll call, and just knowing that they were close by in the men's camp helped me endure the hardships of this horrible place.

More than three thousand Jewish prisoners worked either a twelve-hour day shift or a twelve-hour night shift, and all were overseen by cruel SS men. Workshops for carpenters, knitters, draftsmen, tailors, and other craftsmen had been built to serve the German war machine. Here Jewish slave laborers were used and abused.

As spring turned into summer, suddenly our barracks were invaded by huge rats. The size of mature cats, they ate everything in sight, pieces of food we tried to save for the next day, even our clothing. These rodents were not afraid of people. Night after night they jumped from bunk to bunk consuming everything they could find. The worst were the rat bites. Covering my face with a wash basin, I tried to sleep a few hours a night, but the rats bit my cheeks, hands, and legs no matter how well I tried to cover myself. Things became worse as the weather became warmer. Ultimately nobody could sleep, having to fight the rats all night.

Even the SS realized that under such conditions we were not able to perform the work in the many shops that served the Germans. They decided to exterminate the rats. Since it was summer, they ordered us to leave the barracks for twenty-four hours. We spent the night sitting on the grounds where the daily roll calls took place. The SS put bait and gas inside the barracks to poison the rats. What irony! The gas used to exterminate the rats was the same poison gas, Cyclon B, that was used in Auschwitz-Birkenau to gas the people, but we were not aware of this at that time. Once the rats were killed, we returned to the barracks.

But where did these rats come from? Before the Jewish prisoners were brought to Blizyn, this camp had been for Soviet prisoners of war. Thousands of them were housed here from 1941. Not one of them survived. They were beaten and starved to death. Their bodies were buried in ditches in the forest that surrounded the camp. Rats found their breeding place in these mass graves, consuming the bodies of the prisoners of war. Once there was nothing left of the corpses, the rats came into our camp looking for food.

Prisoners who worked outside the Blizyn camp had to wear the striped prisoners' garb or have a wide red stripe painted on their outer clothing to prevent their escape. Those working inside the camp like my father, brother, uncle, and I wore civilian clothing.

A new transport came to Blizyn in the late summer of 1943. Until now we had people from Radom, Kielce, Czestochowa, Piotrkow, and Tomaszow. The newly arrived men and women came from Bialystok, among them a few doctors. What struck us most about the women from Bialystok were their bandaged wrists. We thought they must have tried to commit suicide.

Most of the women were young and intelligent. When we asked them about their bandaged wrists, they told us their hometown of Bialystok was

Mira's Uncle Henry (Heinrich) Ryczke with his wife, Anni, Danzig, 1931. Henry was killed at the Plaszow camp in 1944.

not far from the Treblinka death camp. Being so close to the place where more than 800,000 Jews were killed, they were fully aware of the exterminations of people by gas. When their ghetto was to be liquidated, and trains were taking Jews from Bialystok to Treblinka, many decided to take their lives. That is what had happened to this transport. Once their train stopped in Treblinka, the young women cut their wrists. They did not want the Nazis to march them to the gas chamber. They preferred to die by their own hands. But when the car they were in was hitched to another locomotive, the women in the cattle car realized they were not being taken to be killed but were being sent somewhere else. So they bandaged their bleeding wrists and survived.

This was the first time we learned the truth about the death camp, about the fate of our dear ones who were sent "east." All my hope that I would see my mother, grandparents, and other relatives again was now gone.

At Blizyn my father and brother worked in the carpenters' shop, my uncle in a leather shop, and I toiled in the camp's laundry. Life in crowded barracks with no sanitation, four of us to a bunk, contributed to the infestation of millions of lice. We did not even have warm water in which to wash ourselves. Only taps with cold water were available for the prisoners. No soap. No towels.

When we first arrived we were taken once a week to the baths, where our lice-infested clothing was taken away and exchanged for clean ones. My job was to wash the clothing so filled with lice that they formed a layer two inches deep on top of the water. But working in the laundry had a special advantage. I could secretly take my father's, brother's, and uncle's clothing to wash as often as needed. I could only do this during the night shift, risking beatings and other punishment if caught. But it was so important to stay clean of lice because this vermin was the cause of typhoid.

In spite of having clean clothing, my father came down with typhoid in March 1944 at the beginning of the camp epidemic and when space was still available in the so-called hospital. Soon, however, the hospital barracks was so overcrowded with typhoid patients that when my brother and uncle became infected with this dreaded disease they had to stay in their assigned barracks. No medication was available. Prisoners either survived or died. With high fever for almost two weeks, very little food, and weakened by hard work, almost 30 percent of the ill died. Fortunately my dear ones survived.

By the end of April I became ill with typhoid, and so did Eva, my girl friend, with whom I shared a bunk. Both of us were so sick, we were unable to swallow any food. We survived only on the black liquid that was called coffee. Lying delirious on our bunk, because there was no room in the hospital, I still recall the camp doctor, Dr. David Wajnapel, coming to see us daily to help us with kind words of encouragement. He had no other help to give. Our bodies either fought the disease or we would succumb.

When the fever broke, the crisis was over and both Eva and I got better. Almost three weeks of lying on the bunk weakened my legs to such an extent that I was unable to walk. My father and brother came to my barracks after roll call to teach me how to walk again. I can still see myself dragged between them and told to first lift one foot, then put it in front of the other. Repeating this exercise with their help, I slowly learned to walk again.

By the time I got well, my place at work was already taken by somebody else. My father was by now working as a bookkeeper for the SS man in charge of the carpenter's shop. A cruel and sadistic man nicknamed "Brillock," because of the thick glasses he wore, became my father's boss. (In German "Brille" means spectacles.) Somehow he developed a liking for my father and put pieces of bread on his desk so that my father could bring additional food to us. But my brother and I were so starved after fighting and surviving typhus that this food was not enough. My father went to the only dentist in camp and asked him to remove the gold bridge from his mouth. This he bartered for some butter and more bread. With this additional food we regained some of the strength we had lost. Knowing that I could not work as hard as before, my father approached "Brillock" to ask whether I could help him in the office with some of the bookkeeping. This notoriously cruel SS man consented, and the next day I went to work at the office. Not only was my job easier, but "Brillock" provided us with food to supplement our meager diet. More food was a blessing for all of us. We were not as hungry as before and could share some of the food with others.

When the typhoid epidemic was at its climax, a few hundred of the prisoners in the camp were ordered to leave for the Plaszow Concentration Camp. Among them was my uncle. Not until after the war did we learn that he was shot just a few weeks after he arrived there.

Our camp commandant was SS Hauptsturmfuehrer Heller, who came to us from Majdanek. He replaced a terribly sadistic SS man, Paul Nell, who with his vicious dog, Pasha, constantly terrorized camp inmates. At the com-

mand of his master this dog tore victims to pieces. Heller, as camp commandant, was ordered to report any changes in the camp to Berlin, especially if
an epidemic broke out. Heller knew that if he reported the typhoid epidemic,
this camp and all its inmates would be liquidated. Because he never sent the
report to Berlin, we were all saved from certain death. When he was caught
by U.S. forces after the war, he was arrested and brought to trial as a former
SS camp commandant. So many of the former Blizyn inmates testified in
his defense that he was set free. Decency and courage could be found even
among the dreaded SS men. Thanks to "Brillock," my father, my brother,
my friend Eva, and I had extra food. Thanks to Heller we in Blizyn were
spared.

Living in filth for fifteen months, being bitten by rats at night, slaving
at work, and living in constant fear—this was life in the Blizyn camp. Soon
this was to end as the Russian front moved closer with each passing day. We
hoped we would remain together, that the Soviets would liberate us. Our
ultimate dream was for the war to end soon. Hope gave us the strength to
endure—to survive.

# Chapter 9

# PINIO

Pinio was an active, lively seven-year-old boy when I saw him for the last time. With his large and wise dark-brown eyes, he looked older than his years. Jewish children in the ghettos and camps shed their childhoods quickly, becoming instant grownups. What adults did not understand was the children's perception and intuition.

An only child adored by his mother and father, Pinio lived two houses away from us. His parents were also residents of Tomaszow Mazowiecki, as were his grandparents. The family had operated its own hardware store on Warszawska Street before the Germans ordered their property to be handed over to Aryan owners. Pinio's father joined the Jewish ghetto police. A man of principle and great integrity, he did it to protect his family from deportation.

Then came the day when the Tomaszow ghetto was liquidated, its inhabitants sent to the Treblinka death camp. Pinio and his parents were spared, unusual because very few children remained with their parents. The lucky ones were children of ghetto officials. Of the remaining Jews, everyone had to work now. Pinio went to work with his mother at the Dietz factory. His job was to sweep the floor.

Life returned almost to a normal routine. I worked with Pinio's mother in the factory and watched Pinio growing up. The lull was short-lived. While we worked in the factory, others had to pack and crate belongings of the deported Jews. Once the job was finished, we, the remaining Jews of Tomaszow, were sent to a concentration camp. With little warning, we were ordered to pack our few personal items and to board cattle cars that took us to the Blizyn Camp.

Our lives in this concentration camp were completely transformed. Men and women were separated. Children went with their mothers. Pinio and his mother stayed in my barracks. Here we slept on bare wooden planks without blankets or pillows. Many of us slept in the clothing we wore during the day in order to protect it. During the nights clothing was often stolen, especially shoes, which could be bartered for food. Our daily rations were so meager that to supplement our diet we had to barter what we still had: a ring or watch, even gold fillings from a person's teeth. The Ukrainian guards were eager to provide us with some bread, potatoes, or sugar for our few treasures.

The endless hours of standing at roll calls in the mornings and evenings, no matter what the weather, were torture. Our camp commandant, SS Lieutenant Nell, made daily rounds, always accompanied by his dog. This vicious animal was trained to attack Jews and, at Nell's command, tear them to pieces. Cries and screams of his defenseless victims could be heard throughout the camp. We were petrified and sped up our work whenever the warning of the approaching Nell was whispered.

One misty autumn day in 1943 during roll call, the women were ordered to remain standing after the counting of prisoners was completed. Then came the order: "Mothers, bring your children to the center of the camp. We will take them to a better place. They will be provided with more food and will work at lighter chores." These were the words of Commandant Nell.

After he had spoken, nobody moved. Not one of the mothers stirred. Suddenly the children tore away from their mothers and began to run into the barracks to hide. Mothers, in their desperation, ran after them, dragging the screaming children to the SS officers.

Then I saw Pinio. He too ran back into the barracks, but was apprehended by his mother. "They are lying to you. They are going to kill us," he cried. His eyes were the eyes of a hunted and terrified animal. In his innocence he sensed the imminent danger that awaited the children. His mother tried to calm him, to pacify her frightened son. She took his hand and calmly walked her only child to the group where more than twenty children were surrounded by the SS.

We stood motionless and watched with horror as mothers bid farewell to their children. I saw in Pinio's eyes a look I shall never forget. Those dark eyes looked back at us as the SS officers marched the children away to the waiting bus. All of us were paralyzed. We heard the bus leave, then were ordered to report to work. Cries and lamentations of the mothers were heard all day long. In spite of our own doubts, we tried to reassure them, telling the mothers that their children would be safe.

Then came evening, and another roll call. When we were dismissed, the fate of the children spread like the wind. Once in the bus, the SS drove them to a forest not far from the camp and with machine guns killed all of them. A group of men from our camp told us that ditches had been prepared for this special "action." Their task was to bury the children and level the ground so no traces would be left.

Mothers and fathers could not believe what they were told. They wanted to believe their children were alive and safe. But soon all of us realized how deceived we were by the SS.

I could not stop thinking of Pinio and his words. I thought to myself, "He was right. He knew the truth." His sad, dark eyes still haunt me.

*Chapter 10*

# CHOOSING LIFE

"In a few days this camp will become part of the Majdanek Concentration Camp." The announcement was made in November 1943 while we, the inmates of the Blizyn Camp, stood at attention during roll call.

Rumors had come true. For weeks SS guards had hinted that our camp would become part of Majdanek. We heard about the horrors of this large camp: the constant executions, the tortures, and the gas chambers. Now we too would become prisoners of this dreaded place.

Not that being imprisoned at Blizyn was a paradise. Blizyn was a cruel camp. We, the prisoners, worked until we succumbed to disease or hunger. Some of us worked twelve-hour shifts for the war industries; others worked twelve-hour shifts inside the camp. What changes would take place? Would the Nazis ship all of us to Majdanek? Would I be separated from the only family I had left after almost my whole family had perished at Treblinka? The thought of losing my father, brother, and uncle, of being torn from them, sent shivers of fear through my body. The remaining four of us had endured so much. We grieved and mourned our losses, and our only hope was to stay together for support.

In Blizyn men and women lived in separate barracks, but we saw each other after roll call each evening. My father and my brother were my constant source of encouragement and strength. Would I be able to continue without them? I knew I needed them.

At this time I worked the night shift in the camp laundry, a horribly depressing job. I continued washing prisoners' clothing, which was infested with millions of lice. A two-inch layer of the vermin always floated on top of the water as I worked. Some of the lice drowned, but many remained in the seams of the clothing and never died. I took the wet garments to a separate drying room where a primitive dryer was operated by prisoners.

A good friend of mine also worked on the night shift and operated the dryer, and we discussed the changes that would take place in our camp. We had known each other since the ghetto years, and I knew his wife and young son who had been killed at Treblinka. Ours was a true friendship, and we could talk freely about anything. He, too, was horrified that soon our camp would become part of Majdanek, and he voiced his anxieties.

When I returned after a few hours with a second load of wet clothes to be dried, he shocked me with a proposal: Would I consider taking my own life? His exact words. "I love you, and if I cannot live with you, I want to die with you." Until that moment suicide had never entered my mind. I wanted to live, not die. I told my friend that I would need a few days to think about it. He warned me that we might not have much time left. Any day could bring the changes we were so afraid of. But I needed time.

Instead of sleeping during the day after the long night shift, I tried to sort out my thoughts and feelings. How could I hurt my dear father and brother by taking my life? How much pain would this act of mine inflict upon them? It would certainly crush them morally. Judaism does not allow taking one's own life, but these times are not normal. Am I being selfish by even considering suicide? On the other hand, could I endure life if I were to be separated from my father and brother?

An inner voice told me: "You must live, no matter how hard life will be." I was only twenty; the best years of my youth had been spent in ghettos and in this miserable camp. Yet deep inside me was the will and strong desire to live. I did not want to die.

The following night, while taking the clothes to the dryer, I told my friend that I really did not want to consider suicide and gave him all the reasons. He had come equipped with a hypodermic needle and explained to me that by injecting air into our veins, it would be so easy to die. I was still scared and uncertain about what to do.

The temptation was strong. We could end all the torments and suffering right here. But I did not listen. Instead, I tried to dissuade him, give him hope, and try to make him see that it was our duty to live. Listening patiently to my words, he asked me to take one more day to think it over.

When we reported to roll call the next morning, our camp was already part of Majdanek. New SS guards and a new camp commandant took charge, and life in our camp did not undergo many changes. By hesitating, by listening to my inner voice, we chose life.

My friend and I survived the war. We each married someone else, had children, and built new lives.

# Chapter 11

# A PLACE CALLED AUSCHWITZ

"Auschwitz, Auschwitz! We are being sent to Auschwitz." On July 27, 1944, this was the cry heard throughout the Blizyn Concentration Camp.

Most of the three-thousand-plus Jewish prisoners had been here for almost two years, having previously lived under the Nazis in crowded ghettos. Hunger, illness, and weakness had taken their toll. The mortality rate had been horrendous, but I still had my father and brother with me. Now we faced the unknown—a place called Auschwitz.

The war had turned to Hitler's disadvantage. The Soviets were pushing west, and the Americans and British had landed in France. Germany needed all of its men, young and old, to defend the Fatherland. They needed us, their slaves, to work for Germany's war machine. As long as we had the strength, we were to repair roads and bridges, dig ditches, and work in factories. This was the reason the order was given to evacuate us to Auschwitz. Carrying what was left of our few personal possessions, we were marched to the waiting cattle cars. I still felt lucky because my father, brother, and friend, Eva, were with me.

For three days and three nights we sat in the dirty, crowded cattle car. In blazing heat, with little water and almost no food, we endured the journey into the unknown. In one corner of the car the Nazis placed a huge bucket into which we could relieve ourselves. With more than 80 people in the car, it filled quickly. Whenever the train stopped, the SS opened the door long enough to allow men to take out the bucket overflowing with human waste. Some always spilled on the floor, causing a horrible reeking smell. Everyone tried to get to a small opening near the sliding door to get a little fresh air. The journey seemed endless with so many stops along the way to allow military trains to pass. We prayed for it to end soon. This was the route to Auschwitz.

On the evening of the third day, the train stopped. Through the cracks of the car walls we saw a platform filled with men in striped prisoner's clothing. We heard many voices, mostly shouting in German. We also heard dogs barking. Not knowing what to expect, many pushed to be the first ones out when the doors opened. As we exited the cattle cars, men and women were ordered separated, with children to go with their mothers.

I embraced my father and brother, promised to take care of myself, and with tears running down my cheeks, kissed both of them. They stepped to the right, and I went to the left. I can still see my tall sixteen-year-old brother looking at me from the gates to Birkenau. This was the last time I saw him.

I marched with the column of women through the camp gate accompanied by camp police called Kapos. One Kapo, a young girl, marched next to me, and told me that I reminded her of her sister. She was from Hungary; I was from Danzig. She said she had lost most of her family in Auschwitz; then she asked, "Are you hungry?" I was starved. I hadn't eaten in two days. She reached into her pocket and handed me a piece of bread. For me it was a miracle—a complete stranger sharing her food. At that time I was unaware of the rules of Auschwitz. Kapos were the privileged prisoners who received more and better food—they were camp elite.

This girl answered many questions we had about Auschwitz. From her we learned that we were in the part called Birkenau, as were most Jewish prisoners. "You are fortunate," she told us. "You are being taken to a real bath house." We, the newly arrived, did not understand. "Why do you say we are lucky?" I asked. Then we were told the truth about this place. She pointed to the many tall chimneys belching out dark smoke. "From the platform where you arrived, most Jews are taken directly to the gas chambers and their bodies are burned in one of four crematoria. Most Jewish transports never enter the camps of Auschwitz. They are taken to be killed as soon as they arrive. This is what happened to my family," she explained. Now we understood what Auschwitz was.

We stopped in front of a large barracks—the bath house. As we waited outside we saw columns of people marching slowly toward the gas chambers. Young and old, men and women and children, walked in complete silence. They were unaware of the imminent death awaiting them. "Is this where my father and brother will go? Will they die in the gas chambers of Auschwitz?" I wondered. They were the only family I had left. Then I became aware of the horrible stench in the air—the smell of burning human flesh. I have never forgotten that smell.

Once admitted into the bath house, all our clothing, shoes, and personal possessions were taken from us. Under penalty of death we were forbidden to keep money, jewelry, photos, or papers. Our heads and bodies were shaved in a brutal way by SS men. Naked and scared we were ordered into the showers. Without soap or towels, we stood under ice-cold water. Wet and cold we emerged on the other side, given striped prisoner's clothing, no underwear, no stockings or socks, no belts. Wooden clogs instead of leather shoes barely fit me. They were much too large, and I had a hard time walking, but this is how we were marched to our barracks, or "Block" in German. Desperate, cold, and hungry, we still managed to joke about the way we looked—like unrecognizable monsters.

Our barracks was managed by a "Blockaelteste" from Slovakia. A seasoned and longtime Auschwitz prisoner, she did not spare the whip on us. I was given a place on the middle tier where five of us had to sleep on bare wood without blankets, pillows, or mattresses. When one of us turned, all had to turn. But this first night in Auschwitz, nobody slept. We were all in shock as we perceived the truth of this place.

At 5 A.M. the whistle blew. Again we were told to hurry to assemble at the front of the barracks for morning roll call. Although it was July, we shivered as we stood at attention for hours in the cold morning air for the counting of thousands and thousands of prisoners in all the Auschwitz camps. Once roll call was over, we were given our meager morning ration—a black liquid, so-called coffee, and a small piece of dark, heavy bread. Because bread was given us by weight, it was made heavier by adding sand and ground glass, and barely satisfied our gnawing hunger. Next we were told that we, the lucky ones, those who could work, would have a number tattooed on our left arms. The tattooing process was slow and painful, physically and psychologically. Until now we had our names; everything else had been taken from us. Now we were mere numbers. On July 31, 1944, I became A-15744. Using the alphabet helped the Nazis camouflage the actual number of camp prisoners.

Then, treated like subhumans, we were sent to perform many different jobs. Hitler's goal was to take away our humanity, reduce us to nameless and senseless creatures. To the Nazis we were vermin; our lives did not matter. For as long as they could work us, we lived. Those who became sick or too weak to perform went to the gas chambers. Selections were conducted almost daily, with Dr. Mengele choosing who lived and who died. I lived through many selections, but I will never forget the anxiety, fear, and horror I endured.

How did I survive? With the help of God, the support of friends, kind deeds by those who shared food with me. We were determined to go on, to retain our humanity, to live despite the danger and obstacles. But most of all the will to outlive our enemies gave me and my friends the inner strength to survive. Auschwitz was a creation by people who wanted to rule the world by terror and hate. Because of Auschwitz the world will never be the same. Auschwitz was absolute evil and a warning of what mankind is capable of doing.

# Chapter 12

# A PROMISE KEPT

The eastern front was moving closer each day. Would the Soviets advance quickly enough to liberate us? The SS guards yelled across the barbed wire, "Soon all of you will be exterminated." They knew that orders from Himmler were specific: all Jewish inmates of concentration camps were to be killed before the advancing Allied troops could free them.

As previously told, most inmates were ordered to evacuate the Blizyn-Majdanek Camp in July 1944. Although we didn't know it, as a family my father, brother, and I were together for the last time. We were still in the cattle car destined for Auschwitz. To us the name meant just another concentration camp. Little did we know that no other camp could compare with the hell that was Auschwitz. In spite of the misery we were in, we tried to talk about a better tomorrow and to comfort each other.

Until now, I had been able to keep a few mementos, such as family photographs. My father still had important papers and addresses of friends. He noticed the tin canteen I was holding, which still had some food in it. Suddenly my father said, "Hand me the canteen. We will put all the photos and papers inside and you will carry it with you until the war is over."

Without a word, we consumed the food still in the canteen. We ate the stale bread we had saved for this trip. When it was empty, I handed it to my father. Among the papers my father wanted to save were his driver's license, his membership card from the Danzig Grain Exchange, his address book filled with names of friends and relatives abroad, and his last tax return from Danzig in 1938. I added all the photographs that I kept since we left Danzig and closed the canteen. While others in the cattle car were trying to hide money, gold, or jewels, our treasure was a different kind. We had nothing else left.

Whatever jewels we once had were gone long ago. Since the outbreak of the war in 1939 we had been forced to barter everything we owned for bread or potatoes in order to survive hunger in ghettos and camps. I was so proud that my father had entrusted me with the task of holding on to our possessions. I took the canteen from him with the promise that I would guard it and return it to him after the war.

The train was slowing down because we were near our destination, Auschwitz-Birkenau. Through the narrow openings in the cattle car we saw Polish peasants working in the fields. They looked at our train and pointed toward the ground. They knew our probable fate where we were being taken, but we didn't understand what they tried to tell us. They knew the truth about Auschwitz.

"Raus, alle raus!" (out, all out) was the deafening shout as we jumped out. Camp police with whips did not spare anyone who was unable to get out as quickly as ordered. I could not see my father, who was so much shorter. All I could see was my tall brother. "Where are they taking us? Would we ever see each other again?" I thought. I felt so desolate. They stepped to the right, and I went to the left.

Women were now separated into groups. We young ones were marched to the bath house, while the older women and those with children were kept behind. Darkness had descended by the time we were marched toward the bath house. A terrible smell filled the air. We soon learned that it came from the crematoria where the bodies of gassed Jews were burned. Now we understood what Auschwitz was—a death camp for our people.

Verein Danziger Getreide= und Warengroßhändler E.V.

Mitgliedskarte Nr.

für Herrn .......... *Moritz Rycke*

Danzig, den .......... *5. März* .......... 19 ....

Jahresbeitrag Gulden .......... *20.—* für 193 ....

Der Vorstand

Gilt gleichzeitig als Bescheinigung für die erfolgte Beitragszahlung für das laufende Geschäftsjahr

Rudolf Witt

Mira's father's membership card for Grain and Wholesale Merchants in Danzig, issued March 5, 1937.

When we reached the bath house in Birkenau, we were told to undress, leave everything we possessed behind, and line up for the shaving of our bodies and heads. The process of shaving was another torture. SS men did it in a brutal and humiliating way. The razors were dull and the pain was excruciating. The shaved ones were pushed into the shower room. When my turn came, I was stopped at the door by an SS woman. "What are you carrying? You are not allowed to take anything with you!" were her words. Without hesitating, looking straight at her, I said, "My soup. I have my soup in the canteen." An angel must have watched over me. The SS woman believed me, and I entered the shower room with my treasures. Had she ordered me to open the canteen, it would have been the end of me.

The cold shower sobered my senses. "Luck was with me this time," I thought, "but what would happen later? Would I be able to save my canteen again and again?" Only my dearest girlfriend, Eva, knew my secret. She gave me her only pictures of her family to keep with mine. I could not sleep that night, thinking how to save the contents of the canteen.

The next day, my friend Eva and I searched for old rags, pieces of paper, anything to cover and protect our treasure. From then on, whenever we were told that we would be taken to the bath house, I poured soup over the rag-covered papers. A few times I had to open the canteen, but always there was soup on top and the contents were well hidden underneath.

Until the end of the war I lived in constant fear that someone might find out the truth about the hidden papers and pictures and denounce me to the SS. For nine months I risked my life to keep the promise given to my father to protect what was so important to our family. Clinging to these precious items helped give me the courage to hope that soon I would be with my father and brother again.

Liberation found me in the dreaded Bergen-Belsen camp. I began the search for my father and brother. Three months after liberation my father and I were reunited. At first I was so overjoyed to have my father with me that I completely forgot about the canteen. Then I remembered and asked my father whether he recalled our last moments in the cattle car and what I had promised him. "I remember the canteen and I know it was impossible to keep anything personal in Auschwitz. Forget the promise—I did not know what Auschwitz was."

Then I showed him the canteen. Only by miracles was it saved. Many of the photographs were damaged because I had so often covered them with soup. But they were safe now. My father's tax document proved very important after the war when Germany made restitutions to Jews. With it he could prove the income he had before the war. I had guarded the canteen with my life so that I could keep my promise.

In retrospect, I know that guarding the canteen helped give me a reason to go on, to cling to life, and to outlast the war.

# Chapter 13

# AUSCHWITZ-HINDENBURG

All I could hear was the shrill blowing of the whistle. Then came the loud scream: "Out of your bunks, be dressed and ready for roll call in fifteen minutes," the voice of our "blokowa", the prisoner in charge of the Block, announced. The time was 5 A.M.

I did not have to get dressed; we all slept in our clothes. Five of us in one bunk jumped up, smoothed the clothes we were in, and got outside the barracks for roll call. This was the third roll call in Birkenau (Auschwitz II) for us, the new prisoners from Blizyn. This camp was so large that wherever my eyes could see there were barracks with people lined up in front of them. With each Block housing at least a hundred prisoners, there must have been thousands of us on this August morning.

The air was still, and it was cold even though it was August. We had to stand at attention for the counting of the prisoners. In my thin, striped prisoner's garment I shivered as we waited for the SS Rapportführer to count us. The first counting was done by a prisoner functionary who reported the number of prisoners to the SS. He, in turn, repeated the counting to make sure no mistake was made. Usually roll calls lasted one or two hours. This morning was different. We were told that a selection would take place, so we had to wait for the SS officer in charge of selections. Being so new here, I had no idea what a selection meant. As soon as the news of the forthcoming selection reached the camp, the prisoners who came earlier shared the true meaning of "selection" with us.

Anyone with a handicap, any person with sores on their bodies, swollen legs or faces, persons wearing glasses, and those who walked with a limp would be "selected." These were the prisoners the SS men were looking for. "Selected for what?" That was my question. And the old-timers pointed to the chimneys. "Selected for the gas chambers to go up in smoke," was the answer.

Since my early teens I had worn glasses because of nearsightedness. Immediately I was told by prisoners not just to remove them but to destroy them. I took my glasses, stepped on them, and ground them into the earth where I stood. Then we were told by the old-timers to try to look strong, healthy, and to walk in an upright position when our turn came.

The order to undress came. From the distance we could see other prisoners walking stark naked in front of a group of SS men. Some were taken aside, others returned to their ranks. Then the SS approached our group. The officer conducting the selection was a handsome young man wearing white gloves. Later I learned that this was Dr. Joseph Mengele, known in camp as "The Angel of Death."

One by one we had to march in front of the SS. Some of the women had to turn around and be inspected like cattle brought to market. Most of us were fairly young. No elderly women were in our group. As my turn for the inspection came, my heart was pounding, my mouth getting dry. The horror of not passing the inspection, the fear of being selected for death, was hard to contain. My brain was telling me: walk straight, hold your head high, do not look at them, be calm. At first my steps were shaky, but soon I composed myself and did exactly what my brain told me to do. I passed the inspection.

Because the women I was with were young, only a few were taken out. Their numbers, tattooed on their left arms, were written down by the

SS, and after a few days during roll call their tattoo numbers were called out and these women were marched to the gas chamber. After roll call we were allowed to return to our Blocks, and only then did we get our morning ration: lukewarm black liquid called "coffee" in camp. The remainder of breakfast was black bread that had been handed out the previous night. Most of us ate the bread right away so great were our hunger pangs. Seldom was anything left for the next morning.

Days passed slowly. We lived from one roll call in the morning to the one in the evening. Every four or five hours we were allowed to walk to the latrines, always in groups of five accompanied by a Kapo. Those of us who suffered from diarrhea were unable to wait. We felt deprived of the most elementary human needs and so humiliated. To stay clean under these dehumanizing conditions was impossible. To control my basic human needs became my goal. I had dreams: a clean bed; a warm blanket; a dress without lice; enough water, with soap and towels, to wash my body. Also I dreamed of enough bread to still the constant hunger.

We were tattooed and, as it was done, were told that only the lucky ones who are strong enough to work received tattoos. I considered myself lucky. The first selection was over and I survived. But, "God, let me leave this place," was my prayer. "I will work hard and diligently if only I could leave Auschwitz-Birkenau," I prayed every night, in my heart and in silence: "God, spare me from the agony of constant selections, from mistreatment by Kapos, from breathing the stench of burning bodies being cremated around the clock, from fear, hunger, filth, dehumanization."

All these terrible things made me daydream of better times. During the long hours of waiting for food, going to latrines, anticipating selections, we women talked about our dreams. To stay alert, to retain our sanity, we recalled favorite poems. Most of us talked about our lives before Auschwitz, before Blizyn. The images of our family members were always before our eyes. These recollections, these shared memories, gave all of us the strength to endure.

But some friends did become ill and could not remain in the Block. Yes, there was a hospital, or "Revier," as it was called in all concentration camps. Unfortunately these hospitals were only a collections center for the sick and weak. Every so often the Revier was cleared of all inmates, who were taken to the gas chamber. The orders of the SS were to keep only the able-bodied alive. They would not feed those who were sick, those who were unable to work.

A few days after my arrival I tried desperately to find out what had happened to my father and brother. The men's camp was a long distance from ours, and it was impossible to get any news to or from them. I felt perpetual fear for their safety. I dreamed about them at night and prayed that they should stay together. Knowing my father's resourcefulness and his deep love for my brother, I knew that as long as they were together Benno would be cared for.

After a few weeks I slowly adjusted to the horrible conditions. One morning after roll call we were told to remain at attention. "Would it be another selection?" I asked myself. "Will this never end?" But this time our reason for remaining in front of the barracks was quite different.

For the past two years Auschwitz had become a warehouse for slave labor. Every war industry in Germany could purchase cheap labor from among the prisoners of Auschwitz. Recruiters came from all over, from large and small factories, to get slaves. Every German male was needed at the front or in factories. Most of the healthy Germans were either at the Russian front or fighting in the West. The need for slave labor increased with each month. This was August 1944 when the war in the East was not going well for the Germans. Now they needed slaves to work for their war industries in foundries and welding factories all over Germany.

As we stood at attention, a few civilians and a very thin SS officer approached our group. Three hundred women were needed in factories not far from here. This time the "selection" was to live, not to die. The thin SS man asked, "Who among you can type and know office work?" About thirty women raised their hands. "I worked for four weeks in an office in Blizyn helping my father—raise your hand," I said to myself. I raised my hand. All I knew about typing was the brand of the typewriter in my father's office. As a child he let me play with the keys. I never typed. I never filed. I never wrote a business letter. But I did remember my father dictating letters to his secretary. The SS officer told those with hands up to step forward. Then he pointed to me and asked where I was from. When I told him, "from Danzig," he chose me. I was probably the only one in the group who did not know how to type, yet I was selected.

Where did I get the courage to bluff the Nazis? Why did I raise my hand knowing I was never a typist? Again it was an inner voice that told me to dare the SS. I became very scared. What if they found out I lied to them? I did not realize the gravity of my situation. All I knew was that I wanted to leave Auschwitz and wanted work that would require less physical strength. My body was still weak from typhoid fever. I was thin as a board. To get out of Auschwitz I put my life on the line. Among others chosen were good friends from Tomaszow and Blizyn. I would be with them wherever they sent us.

A quick shower, new striped prisoners dresses, and off we were taken to the camp gate where open trucks awaited us. We stood in the truck as it left the camp filled with the smell of death and fire. The destination was a small Silesian town by the name of Hindenburg. Breathing in the fresh country air during the two-hour ride felt like heaven. The greenery of the countryside and the fields with their poppies and cornflowers presented a picture of absolute beauty. Here was life, tranquillity, and peace. A few miles behind, death was the absolute ruler. What a contrast! All of us wished the ride would last forever.

I was sent to Hindenburg in August 1944 from Auschwitz-Birkenau and was among the fortunate ones selected to work in this satellite camp of Auschwitz. The town of Hindenburg had three factories working for the German military establishment. Most of the women were put to work in the foundry or welding factory. A girl named Trude and I were assigned to the camp office.

The camp was newly built and clean. Three Blocks were set off for women prisoners, one Block for the hospital, with an adjoining room for the camp office. Trude and I worked and slept in the office room. The food was better than in Birkenau, and prisoners had access to daily hygiene. The water was cold, but there was plenty of time allowed for washing. Each prisoner had a bunk with a clean blanket.

The thin SS officer who chose us was Adolph Taube. He became our camp commandant. Known by older prisoners for his sadism and cruelty in Auschwitz, he became my immediate boss. I was told horror stories about his murderous character. He was described as a man who murdered many prisoners and who was feared by Auschwitz inmates. My duty as scribe was to write the daily reports to be sent to Auschwitz. Our camp became known as Auschwitz-Hindenburg, a satellite of the "mother" camp.

From the beginning I was told that the reports I typed had to be perfect. There could be no mistakes. Instead of sleeping at night, I practiced typing. Trude could not sleep because of my typing, but she understood why I was doing it. Fearing to be returned to Auschwitz and probably killed for pretending to know office work, I practiced endless hours. Commandant Taube never found out that the camp Schreiberin (scribe) bluffed; that I did not know how to type or how to write official reports. But I learned quickly. My reports looked neat and the commandant was satisfied.

In November two hundred more women were sent to our camp because the Germans needed more slaves for their factories. Then a group of two hundred men arrived. Mostly professionals, the men came from Bohemia. They were ordered to build more barracks needed for new women prisoners. Our office was too small, and Trude and I moved to one of the newly erected Blocks. Our sleeping quarters were shared with the girls who did cleaning for the SS guards. One beautiful and attractive girl became the commandant's "sweetheart," his personal servant with special privileges.

Concentration camp inmates lost their sex drive as soon as starvation weakened their bodies. Most of the Jews came from camps and ghettos where they had little to eat and thought only of food, not sex. We only tried to obtain another bite of bread, another bowl of soup to still the ever-gnawing hunger pangs in our stomachs.

But this was not the case with Kapos and other privileged prisoners.

They could get plenty of food by requisitioning or stealing it, and their living quarters assured them some privacy. Kapos were able to walk freely from the men's camps into the women's, and many of them had lovers.

The SS created official bordellos for their men and SS guards in the larger camps, and they could seek pleasure and satisfy their lusts in these places. Bordellos contained mostly German and Polish women, and the SS selected the best-looking women they could find. No Jewish women were among them unless they were "passing" as German or Polish. The official policy and strict orders to the SS were to have no sexual contact with a Jewess. Yet, there were exceptions. Some SS men did fall in love with a Jewish prisoner, with deadly results for the Jewess.

From the time Hitler came to power, homosexuals in Germany were persecuted. Many were sent to concentration camps where they had to wear the pink triangle on their outer clothing to identify them. Most of them were also confined to a special section of the camp. Also, among the early women prisoners in Auschwitz-Birkenau were lesbians. The majority of them came to the camp in 1942 mostly from Germany, Slovakia, and Bohemia. Often in the middle of the night SS officials, male or female, would enter a women's barracks to look for girls who were sleeping together. The punishment was public flogging.

The year 1944 was ending. Since early December the weather had been terribly cold and there was a lot of snow. Almost five hundred women lived in unheated barracks with no pillows and only one thin blanket to cover our frozen bodies. By the time we moved into our newly erected Block in Hindenburg, winter was approaching. With walls as thin as paper, the place became bitter cold. To stay warm many girls tried to sleep together for warmth, not because they were lesbians. From the time the commandant's "sweetheart" moved into our sleeping quarters, Adolph Taube would surprise us with nocturnal visits. We knew he wanted to make sure that his "woman" was sleeping alone. These visits frightened us and kept women sleeping alone to avoid punishment.

From the time of my arrival at Hindenburg I never got enough sleep. I was summoned in the middle of the night many times to take dictation from the SS officers. I had to follow their orders day and night. I will never forget one night in November 1944 when I was summoned to the commandant's office. Wearing his officer's cap with the SS insignia and carrying a revolver in his hand, he dictated a letter to me. He was completely drunk and his sentences made no sense. As soon as I entered his office, he told me, "If you ever disclose the text of what I dictate you have eaten for the last time. You will be killed." After I took down his incoherent words, I returned to my Block. This letter had to be typed in secrecy. Nobody could read it. I had to type it right away because the commandant wanted it early in the morning. "Will he remember the crazy things he made me write down?" I wondered. Somehow I typed a letter as best I could and presented it to him in the morning. Not even looking at it, he tore it up. He completely forgot what transpired the night before. This was the price I had to pay for being a scribe, for having a less demanding physical job. The mental anguish and anxieties I lived through were often far worse than hard physical work.

As the year 1944 ended, we, the five hundred women and two hundred men of the Hindenburg camp experienced something unheard of for a concentration camp. With the permission of the camp commandant, prisoners were allowed to present a play. The time was close to Christmas, and the mood of the SS was somber. They already knew of the approaching Soviet army and of their probable fate.

Trude and a few of the Slovakian prisoners were given permission to prepare a play for all of the camp prisoners. Trude based it on the words of a German song about "a Sonya with black eyes, who lost her lover somewhere in Siberia." A few girls sang the song in the sentimental play, and I was asked to recite Goethe's *Erlkoenig,* a poem I remembered from my Danzig school years. The lyrics told of a sad father trying to save his feverish son and at the end arriving with a dead child in his arms. Most who heard it cried. Fathers and mothers among the prisoners had lost their children. But in the end, the afternoon play and poetry gave us a boost and new hope.

When the male prisoners arrived at this camp sometime after the women, an order came from Auschwitz to inoculate all of the prisoners against intestinal typhus (Bauchtyphus), which was caused by impure water. The Nazis feared their own people and German workers in factories might catch this dreaded disease from us.

As soon as the men arrived and were settled in their Block, Ceca, the camp doctor, was ordered to test each of the men for typhus. Cultures were to be taken from the anus of each man and sent to Auschwitz to be tested. To do the job, the doctor needed another person to write down each prisoner's number and put it on the flask with each culture. I was completely unaware of the procedure when Ceca asked me to go with her. I found it to be humiliating and unnerving for the prisoners and for me. They had to let down their pants so Ceca could take the samples. I was afraid my hands would shake and the flasks would be broken or mixed up. Shame did not make me turn away from the men, but a feeling of total dehumanization did.

Then inoculations of all prisoners began, and I was Ceca's record keeper. I told Ceca that since childhood I had very bad reactions to inoculations. She told me, "You are never in touch with Germans in factories. I will write that you received the inoculation without giving it to you." Relieved, I forgot all about it.

Then one day while typing the year-end report to be sent to the main Auschwitz camp, I felt chills. My hands started to shake to such an extent that I could barely finish the report. I felt feverish and my teeth were chattering. I lay down on my bed at the bottom of a three-layer tier. With every hour I felt worse. The thin blanket barely protected me from the chills. Since I was shaking all over I asked my friends to call Ceca. As soon as she saw me, she said, "Mira, you have typhus." I hardly heard what she was saying. I did not grasp the seriousness of my situation. As camp doctor she had to report daily those who were ill and the exact nature of their illness. How could she report a case of typhus when she herself had reported inoculating me? She decided to take me to the hospital block and to diagnose my illness as pneumonia.

The camp hospital had two rooms, one for men and one for women, plus an operating room. Each room had only four bunks. When I came in, only one other woman was in the room. I was hallucinating about food, and so was she. We made up recipes for banquets. She was discharged a few days later and I was in the room alone. For two solid weeks I fought high fever, and was cared for by Ceca. Through the Block window I could see the snow and icicles hanging from the roof. The bitter cold permeated the unheated camp hospital.

Slowly the fever subsided and I was winning the typhus battle. One day Ceca came to tell me that a commission from Auschwitz was in the camp and wanted to see the hospital. Commissions from Auschwitz were always bad news. Two SS men entered the room. They read the chart, looked at me, and told me to show my left arm with my tattoo number. One of them copied the number, and they left. I knew very well what this meant. They would send me to my death in Auschwitz. I was not capable of working any more and did not deserve to live.

Ceca returned when the SS left and we discussed the seriousness of my situation. There was only one way out: leave the hospital and return to my job. I was so weak, even walking was a problem. How would I ever get back to my Block? How would I be able to work? Friends dressed me and almost carried me from the hospital to my Block. Exhausted I lay down on my bunk.

Lagerfuehrer Taube was told that I was back in the Block. He came to see me and what he saw was a ghost. But to my surprise, he told me to take my time and only do what was physically possible. During my illness, Katya from Slovakia did my job. She was a longtime friend of Trude and was ordered to help out. She continued to do most of my work while I tried to regain my strength.

Each day I waited to hear from Auschwitz, but an order for me to leave never came. Two days after my return from the hospital I had a dream. In it I saw my father and lots of snow. My father showed me the heavy shoes he was wearing. Then it all faded away. When I awoke, I told Trude, "I dreamed about my father and I saw shoes. Shoes mean we will walk." Trude and my roommates laughed at my dream interpretation. But I was so sure that my dream would come true that I took an old piece of cloth and made a satchel out of it.

The next night was January 18, 1945. The commandant came into our office and ordered all papers, all documents, destroyed. I stood all night in front of a stove and burned copies of all the reports I had typed with so much pain and anxiety. Early in the morning the order came for all prisoners to line up. We were ordered to leave camp on foot. No transportation was available.

Each one was given a whole loaf of bread to last us for the duration of the march. We could fill our canteens with some of the "coffee," something warm in the 30-degree-below-zero weather. Prisoners were allowed to take their thin blankets for protection from the weather.

I was still so weak that I did not believe I could walk in snow and in such cold temperatures. That moment in my life I really wanted to die. But the order was for all of us to leave the camp. No prisoner was to remain. The Soviet army was already near Cracow, and Auschwitz had ordered its prisoners evacuated from all camps, satellite as well as mother camp. Those unable to walk were to be left behind and shot. In my desperation I approached the commandant to ask, "Please shoot me. I cannot walk." His words were: "You will march. You will survive. I will not shoot you."

Supported by my friends, I managed to leave the Hindenburg camp. The nightmare of the death march began. But Adolph Taube was right. I marched, and I survived. During the five months in Auschwitz-Hindenburg, not one of the prisoners was sent back to Auschwitz, and not one was killed.

# Chapter 14

# EVACUATION AND DEATH MARCH

The whiteness of the snow was blinding. In my misery I saw the road crowded with ghostly figures trying desperately to march swiftly under the cruel orders of the SS. Distinguishing between men and women was difficult. We all looked like walking dead. Some managed to take their blankets with them from camp. With their bodies covered, they at least had some protection against the biting frost of January 1945.

Every so often a shot pierced the ice-cold air. We did not turn around to look, knowing that this would prevent us from keeping up with the column. "Schnell, schnell" were the constant reminders of the SS guards who were watching the endless columns of marching prisoners.

The sides of the road were lined with the bodies of some of those who had marched ahead of us, of those too weak to keep up with the others. The orders to the SS were very direct, very precise: "Prisoners unable to walk, prisoners who stumble or fall are to be shot. Not one of them is to remain alive. Not one of them is to fall into the hands of the approaching Soviet army." These were Himmler's orders given to the SS when concentration camps had to be evacuated. And these orders were followed to the day the war ended.

While passing the bodies of those whose suffering was over, I tried to see their faces. Most of those shot were men. I was afraid to look, but was compelled by some stronger force within me. "Will I see the bodies of my father or brother?" I wondered. I had parted from them at the gates of Auschwitz half a year ago and did not know their fate. Could they have been in one of the columns from Auschwitz that walked this road a few hours earlier? Would I be able to recognize them? All the prisoners had the same dark-gray complexion. I was afraid that I might not even recognize the faces of my own father and brother.

We dragged ourselves along this snow-covered highway. The goal was to reach the city of Gleiwitz, where freight cars were awaiting us. This Silesian panorama with its thousands of walking skeletons reminded me of the picture of the Napoleonic army on its retreat from Moscow. But instead of the dead horses, this road was covered with the bodies of our friends and comrades.

We marched five in a row. Having barely recovered from typhus, my strength was dwindling. I could hardly lift my feet. Wearing the assigned wooden shoes, to which the snow was sticking, every step took more of my strength. My friends were holding me, one by my left arm and one by my right, to prevent me from stumbling and falling. One of the SS guards saw me struggling. He was an older man, a guard at the camp in Hindenburg from which we were evacuated. "Take my extra pair of boots. You will be able to walk better. You can return them to me once we get to Gleiwitz," he said. And he handed me the pair of leather military boots that had been hanging over his left shoulder.

I had no time to think. Should I accept the boots or not? I took them. I put my own wooden shoes into the small bag I was carrying. But after walking for a few minutes in leather boots that kept my feet warm and dry, I became weaker and weaker. It took all my strength just to lift my feet in the heavy military boots. I had no choice but to return them to the guard who tried to help me. But he was nowhere to be seen. He must have walked ahead of our column.

I was desperate. There was no way I could continue walking in the heavy boots, and I could not carry them either. I dropped the German boots on the road and continued to walk in my wooden shoes for two days until we reached Gleiwitz. My friends and I were fully aware that, should the SS guard find out that I discarded a possession of the SS, I would be shot for sabotage. By sheer luck I never saw the man again, but I always remembered that an SS guard tried to help me.

By the time we arrived at the railroad station in Gleiwitz, the men in our group all looked like zombies. Their faces were black and swollen. Those who survived this death march had very little strength left. We, the women, somehow fared better. The freight cars that were waiting to take us to other camps were open coal cars. We boarded them in bitter cold weather, one hundred of us to each car. Squeezed like sardines in a can, we could barely move. Women and men were in separate cars. On snow-covered wooden floors we sat in one position. We were never allowed to leave the car until we reached our destination. Under these horrible conditions we had to relieve ourselves where we sat. Everything under us froze.

For the next ten days snow was our only food and water. The bread we received when we left Hindenburg was gone long ago. Our journey seemed endless. From the names of the stations we passed we knew we were going through Bohemia. People stood some distance from the train with its dreadful-looking cargo. They were strictly forbidden to get close to us or to throw us any food. In the eyes of these strangers we could see pity as well as horror. They were helpless and afraid to ease our suffering.

The train had to stop many times during this journey. Whenever a military train with troops to or from the eastern front passed, our train was moved to other tracks and kept waiting for endless hours. Other trains with prisoners like us passed by. Again I searched to find a familiar face among the male prisoners.

From Bohemia we traveled to Austria and stopped at the Mauthausen

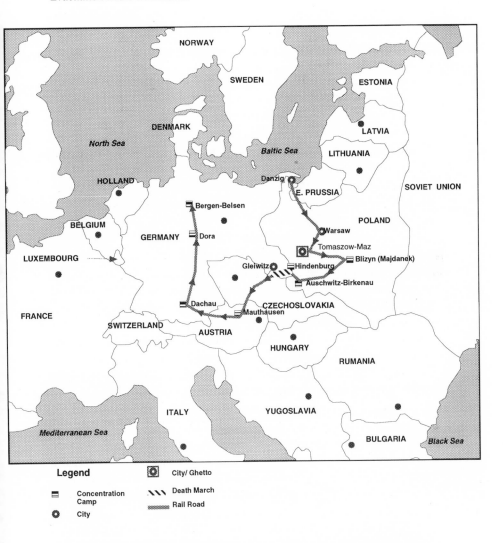

Mira's forced journeys during the Holocaust, October 1939 to April 1945. From Danzig to Warsaw, to Tomaszow-Mazowiecki, to Blizyn-Majdanek, to Auschwitz-Birkenau, to Hindenburg, to Bergen-Belsen.

Concentration Camp. The SS tried to unload the male prisoners, but Mauthausen was already overcrowded, so we had to continue our journey. We entered southern Germany, stopping again at Dachau, but still without being able to unload the male prisoners from our train. Moving north toward Buchenwald, we arrived at the Nordhausen Concentration Camp. Here at the Dora Camp all of us left the train.

Dora was known for its production of the V-1 and V-2 rockets that were used by the Germans against England. Here in the Hartz Mountains, factories were so well concealed that they were never found by Allied bombers. In these mountains prisoners from Buchenwald and Auschwitz were worked to death producing Germany's deadly weapons. As we entered the camp, we saw skeleton-like men hardly able to walk. The death rate among these prisoners was so high, the SS commandant gladly accepted the men that were in our transport. For women there was no work here.

For the first time since we left Hindenburg we were given some bread and soup and allowed to rest overnight. From the many days of walking and later sitting in our own filth we were so dirty, so covered with vermin, that we welcomed the shower that was offered us. By now it was already the end of January and the weather was extremely cold. The shower we were allowed was with ice-cold water. Our clothing was taken from us to be deloused, and in the meantime we waited outside completely naked after the cold shower. That no one dropped dead or contracted pneumonia was a miracle.

The next day all of the women were taken to the railroad station again and put into closed cattle cars. We were told that our destination was the Bergen-Belsen Camp near Celle, where traveling north we soon arrived. As we walked toward the camp, we saw a mountain of dead bodies at the entrance. From our guards we learned that Bergen-Belsen was a camp for internees, not a death camp like Auschwitz.

The sight of so many dead bodies shocked us. Most of the dead were nude, their clothing nowhere to be seen. Soon we understood the reason. The mystery of the nude bodies was solved as soon as we came into the camp.

The death rate at Bergen-Belsen was very high, mostly because of hunger, exhaustion, and disease, and there was only one crematorium to dispose of the dead. Prisoners had to drag the bodies to the gate, but before they did this the clothing of the unfortunate victims was taken by other prisoners. The living had to be protected from the cold. Thus we arrived at the final place. This marked the end of our evacuation from Auschwitz-Hindenburg.

# Chapter 15

# BERGEN-BELSEN

The weather was raw, damp, and cold in February 1945. After almost two weeks in an open coal car following days of marching in the ice-cold, snowy weather, we prisoners arrived at our destination, the concentration camp of Bergen-Belsen. We, the women from Silesia, got out of the cattle cars to walk into the camp. On the road were signs: to Lueneburg. This helped me know the camp was located in northern Germany somewhere between Hannover and Lueneburg. The camp was just a few kilometers from the railroad station of Bergen.

What kind of a camp was Bergen-Belsen? We were told that it was a detention, not a death camp. Before it became a concentration camp, Jews who were to be exchanged for Germans in other countries were brought here to be taken to neutral countries. But this was not the case now. Not a death camp, we were told, yet we saw corpses all over. In fact, a mountain of dead bodies greeted us as we entered. No, there were no gas chambers, but the mortality rate from starvation, cold, disease, and beatings was so enormous that the one crematorium located near the camp could not dispose of all the bodies.

Exhausted, hungry, and cold, we were taken inside Bergen-Belsen. As we were marched to the barracks that would house us, we saw women prisoners who looked like skeletons with swollen faces and hollow eye sockets. We were stopped with questions: "Where did you come from? What was the last camp you were in? Did you by chance know my sister, my mother?" Many wanted to know our hometowns. Everyone wished we had some word of their relatives.

One of the women heard me say that my hometown was Danzig. "You are lucky," she said. "Here in Bergen-Belsen one of the kitchen Kapos is from Danzig." How strange, I thought. Would I meet someone I knew from my hometown in this God-forsaken place?

Danzig had more than ten thousand Jews before the war. The chances I would meet someone I knew were very slim. Yet, I asked the woman, "What is the Kapo's name?" "Elsie" (not her real name), she replied. I could not believe my ears. In 1937—just eight years ago—when I still lived a normal life with my family in Danzig, a girl by this name was in the Zionist Youth group to which I belonged. I remembered her vividly. She had pitch-black hair in braids and small eyes. She was the only girl by this name I had known in Danzig. Could she be here? For days I thought about her but was much too weak to try to find her.

The barracks we occupied had no beds. We had to sleep on the bare floor. More than two hundred women were crowded into the space. The walls were covered with frost. The floors were covered with dirt and human feces. When we lay down to sleep at night, we were packed like sardines in a can, as tight against each other as possible. This way we could at least keep a little warmer. All of us slept for weeks in the lice-covered clothing we wore. There were no washing facilities here, and our bodies were covered with sores from scratching. Many of us had infections, with no choice but to endure our miseries. My feet were frostbitten from the long march in the snow during the evacuation from Hindenburg. I could not wear my wooden shoes, so I searched for old pieces of rags or paper to wrap my feet.

After the early morning roll call, most of us returned to the barracks. None of us was fit to work. With hunger and bad weather making our lives unbearable, I remembered the girl from Danzig. If she was truly the one I knew, and if she is a Kapo in the kitchen, should I ask her for help? I knew from the many years in camps that working in the kitchen meant *life*. A Kapo could eat some of the food that was prepared there, could even smuggle out a potato or turnip to help someone. But first of all I had to make sure she was the girl I knew.

One day I went outside the barracks to the kitchen block. From a distance a saw a familiar figure. The girl I knew from Danzig was standing in front of the kitchen door. She had the same pitch-black, thick hair. Should I or should I not go talk to her? I debated with myself. Can I allow pride to take over and disregard my constant hunger pangs? Finally, I decided to try to talk to her. Maybe she could find some work for me in the kitchen. Kapos had powerful positions in concentration camps. They could be helpful and some were.

I went up to the girl and said, "I remember you. I know you lived in Danzig. I too am from Danzig. Do you remember that you and I once belonged to the same Zionist Youth group? We attended the same meetings. I remember that you moved to Danzig from Silesia. Can you help me get a job in the kitchen? As you see, I am very weak. I've just recovered from typhus."

Her answer was, "I do not know you. I do not remember you, and I cannot help you." That was it. Humiliated and desperate, I returned to my barracks and told my friends about the experience. I cried for the first time. All the years in camp I could not cry, but the shame and the hopeless situation I now faced made the tears flow. I regretted that I asked for help.

Then, out of the blue, a young girl who was with me in Hindenburg came looking for me. "Mira," she said, "I have friends from my hometown in Slovakia in charge of a Block not too far from here. They are sisters, and they need a scribe. Are you willing to work for them?" God must have been watching over me. Here I was at the end of my strength, and suddenly I have a chance to get out of this horrible barracks.

I ran to the Block my friend told me about, introduced myself to the sisters, and was "hired" on the spot. My duties consisted of counting the prisoners in the morning and evening, and accompanying working groups to and from their assigned places. At least now I had a bed to sleep in and did not have to sleep on the bare, dirty floor. The sisters also gave me a little more bread and additional soup each day. These were life-saving benefits. Without this extra food I never could have survived. What I did not anticipate was the sadism of these two Slovakian women. They hit and beat prisoners unmercifully and constantly insulted or screamed at me. But to quit this job would mean to starve again, to sleep on a wet, cold, dirty floor, to return to a state of desperation. I decided to endure the insults.

One day when I was taking a group of women to their workshops, a tall, thin woman came up to me. "I heard that you are from Danzig," she said. "For years I came to Zoppot in summers with my husband and children. I am all alone now. I have lost everyone. Can you tell me your name? Maybe I knew your family." I told her my name, and she said she remembered playing cards with my mother in Zoppot. She even remembered my mother's name and our Danzig address. We promised to see each other again, but we never did. She died not long after our conversation.

Meeting her turned my thoughts to my dear mother again. She had perished in the gas chambers of Treblinka. I wondered how much she suffered before she died. Would she have been able to survive a week under these terrible camp conditions? Would her poor health have contributed to a quick death? Would she look as tragic and emaciated had she lived as did the woman with whom she once played cards? A terrible feeling came over me. I was glad that my mother did not have to struggle with the horrors of concentration camp life.

As hard as it is to believe, one of my friends from Tomaszow, who had also been with me in Blizyn and Hindenburg, gave birth to a baby girl. Yes, in this hell on earth a baby was born. I knew about Lolka's pregnancy since September 1944. While in the Hindenburg camp, we had to undergo monthly examinations. Physicians or nurses did not conduct these painful gynecological examinations, but so-called hospital attendants, in reality rough SS men. When we arrived in Hindenburg, Lolka suspected she was pregnant. (Women did not menstruate because of such poor nutrition, so they could not know immediately that they were pregnant). By November she was sure she was carrying a child. We knew she would be sent to Auschwitz and gassed if the SS found out. So we took turns taking her place and giving her prisoner number to the SS each time an examination was held. These men did not see us as individuals, only numbers. Ceca Imre, the camp doctor and my friend, was of great help. Now in Bergen-Belsen, she was in the same barracks as Lolka, and helped deliver her baby daughter. Since all pregnant Jewish women were sent to the gas chambers in Auschwitz-Birkenau, we took the risk to save Lolka.

While we were still in the ghetto, love had flourished. Married couples still lived together, and babies were born. Young people formed unions. Some asked to be married by a rabbi. Then there were couples in love, but who did not think the time was right for a permanent union. Nothing was permanent anymore. Young men were sent away to work at forced labor, and most of them never returned. Many opportunities presented themselves for young people to seek love in spite of the crowded living conditions—in cellars, in attics. Whenever some privacy could be found couples were making love. Once rumors about possible deportation spread, and many couples wanted to marry immediately. As long as there was life in the ghetto, there was also love.

Abortions became quite prevalent, young couples being afraid to bring babies into such an uncertain world. But in spite of the gloomy future, many Jewish babies were born. Unfortunately, all of them went with their mothers to the death camp in Treblinka once the ghetto was liquidated.

After the liquidation of the ghetto, when most of the remaining men and women lost their partners, new liaisons were formed. Lolka and Hesiek became close after both lost their families during the ghetto liquidation. We had no rabbis left, and the young people didn't care anymore about marriage. Such was the case with Lolka and her "husband" Hesiek. In our eyes they were married. They loved each other very much. When we were sent to the concentration camp of Blizyn, Lolka and Hesiek were separated. She came to stay in the same barracks to which I was sent. Hesiek went to the men's barracks. The SS issued a strict order. Any man found in the women's barracks, any woman found in the men's barracks will be shot.

Those who were officially or unofficially married found this very hard. Some men risked their lives to spend an hour with their spouses, especially when days were longer. They knew that the moment it got dark the barracks would be closed. So they stole a few precious moments to be with the ones they loved, then went to their assigned barracks. This is how Lolka and Hesiek were meeting. We, their friends, were on the watch for approaching danger for them. This is how Lolka became pregnant. After the war, Lolka learned that Hesiek had been killed shortly before. He died not knowing that he had a child.

Remembering that his parents, whom she thought of as her in-laws, had emigrated to Palestine before the war, she went there with her baby daughter. Eventually she married. Her daughter, born in a dirty barracks in Bergen-Belsen, is now a grandmother living in Israel. Lolka died in 1993.

When I visited Israel in the early 1980s, I saw Lolka and her family. My husband and I were there and were asked to participate with four other survivors in a torch-lighting ceremony in Jerusalem. Naturally we were all eager to learn about each other. The usual questions were asked: "Where was your home before the war? What was your maiden name? What school did you attend? What youth organization did you belong to?" One of the surviving women told me she was from Polish Silesia, and learning that I lived in Danzig, told me that she too lived there for some time. She could not remember the school she attended, nor the street where she lived. I wondered if she by chance knew the girl who was also from Silesia and in my Zionist Youth group but somehow had no chance to ask.

The evening ceremony was extremely emotional. The lighting of the six flames was followed by a movie about the fate of Jewish children during the Holocaust. My husband, Max, had lost his eight-year-old daughter from his previous marriage. I lost my younger brother. The painful memories came back.

The following day, mentally exhausted, my husband and I were recuperating from the painful torch-lighting event as we sat in the hotel coffeehouse. The same well-dressed woman from Polish Silesia came up to us. Now I had a chance to ask whether she knew the young girl named "Elsie." "Why do you want to know?" she asked. I told her about the girl I knew in Danzig and about my encounter with her in Bergen-Belsen. She looked at me hard when I finished my story, then finally said, "I am Elsie."

My husband turned white. I was speechless. Did I have any premonition that she was the girl from Danzig? What made me tell her this story? She did not look at all like the girl I knew, and her name was not the same. Here was a blonde woman by another name, yet she and the girl I knew were the same person. To meet again in Jerusalem was an unbelievable experience. Life is truly stranger than fiction.

# Chapter 16

# LIBERATION

Spring arrived early in 1945. With the unusual warm weather the misery of our daily lives intensified. Unable to wash our bodies, the lice multiplied from day to day. The morale in the Bergen-Belsen Concentration Camp was at its lowest. Most of us had dysentery and diarrhea. Unable to make it to the latrine in time, we were forced to soil ourselves. We had no paper to clean ourselves, but with warmer weather ahead of us, we dared use part of our clothing to wipe feces from our legs.

This was the most humiliating time in the camp, the most dehumanizing. We tried so desperately for all those years of camps to retain our humanity, our dignity. Now this was gone too.

With April approaching, I decided to leave the Block I worked in. The brutality of the two Slovakian sisters who were in charge of the Block became unbearable. They dealt out beatings and cursed the prisoners constantly. Most of the young women were from Greece. They did not speak or understand German, and because of this, misunderstood the orders given by the two "blokowas."

By now the workshops were out of operation. I did not have to accompany anyone to or from work. Only during roll call in the morning and evening did I have to count the prisoners. The rest of the day was spent roaming around the camp looking for a potato or a blade of grass. We were given less and less food, and resorted to eating whatever we could find. This was an added reason most of us were sick with diarrhea.

With my friend Annemarie, who was also from Danzig, I found a barracks where we wanted to stay. Officially it was prohibited to move from one place to another, but by now the system had broken down and the SS did not pay too much attention to where we lived. Annemarie and I decided to move into a Russian barracks. No sooner did we move in, we were told to give up part of our clothing in exchange for a bunk. We tried another place. Here we had to sleep on the bare floor. The constant going to the latrine and the lack of food made us so weak we could barely walk. During the night many of our friends died in their sleep. We woke up in the mornings, touched the hands of our immediate neighbors. Often they were ice cold. We lived now among the dead. With each day more and more of the prisoners died. There were days when we envied those who died. Their suffering was over. How long would we be able to go on?

From the far distance we could hear the air raids. We could hear the bombs exploding, but did not know who was dropping them. We had no concept of time. The weather was our only calendar. Then one day in April 1945 we were told during roll call that only the SS and the kitchen help could use the water from the pump in the women's camp. SS guards were patrolling the pump around the clock, and anyone who dared get close was shot. We learned soon that the water line from Hannover to our camp had been damaged by British bombs. With increasingly warm weather, the thirst in the camp grew from day to day. Many of us resorted to drinking our own urine. Hunger was painful, but the thirst was excruciating. Women tried to drag themselves near to the pump to get some of the wet sand into their mouths. Instantly they were shot. I had so little strength left I knew our days were numbered.

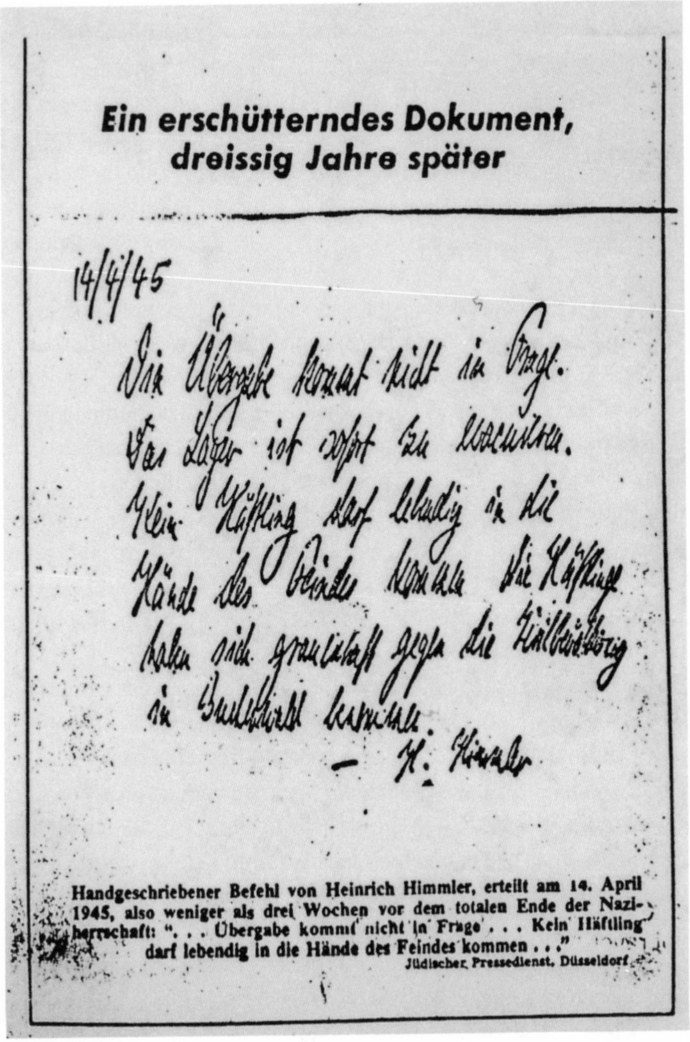

**Ein erschütterndes Dokument, dreissig Jahre später**

14/4/45

Die Übergabe kommt nicht in Frage.
Das Lager ist sofort zu evacuieren.
Kein Häftling darf lebendig in die
Hände des Feindes kommen. Die Häftlinge
haben sich grauenhaft gegen die Zivilbevölkerung
in Buchenwald benommen.

— H. Himmler

**Handgeschriebener Befehl von Heinrich Himmler, erteilt am 14. April 1945, also weniger als drei Wochen vor dem totalen Ende der Naziherrschaft: ". . . Übergabe kommt nicht in Frage . . . Kein Häftling darf lebendig in die Hände des Feindes kommen . . ."**

Jüdischer Pressedienst, Düsseldorf

Orders signed by Heinrich Himmler, head of the SS, April 14, 1945. "The surrender is out of the question. . . . No prisoner should fall into the hands of the enemies alive."

In the meantime there were rumors that we might leave that camp, that soon there would be an evacuation. Prisoners were arriving in Bergen-Belsen from other camps, and transports of prisoners were beginning to leave this camp. There was confusion, and we were petrified with fear. Knowing Himmler's order that no prisoners should fall into the hands of the Allied army alive, we expected the worst. One of the rumors was that the SS put mines around the camp ready to blow us up before the camp could be liberated.

One day we noticed that guards manning the watchtowers wore strange uniforms, not the uniforms of the SS. Who was guarding us now, we wondered? Then came a day of complete silence. An eerie feeling came over the whole camp. No SS people were to be seen. The pump in the camp was not guarded anymore. Finally we could get to it, but only to discover that there was no water left. The pump was dry. The kitchen still had some supplies, but the only food we were getting now was the dark liquid—the so-called camp coffee. Prisoners were stealing bread from the kitchen warehouse, but only the strong ones were able to get it. We could only watch prisoners fighting for some of the bread. For the weaker ones like my friend and me there was nothing left.

On the second day of silence we heard a strange noise from far in the distance. As it grew louder and louder we recognized the sound of approaching tanks. But were these friendly tanks or the SS coming back to kill us all? We did not know until finally we could see the insignia and know the soldiers were not German. It was the sweetest sound and the most beautiful sight when the British tanks surrounded the Bergen-Belsen Camp. But what they saw was a sight for which they were not prepared.

Even in battle these soldiers had not experienced what their eyes now saw: the sight of living dead, of mounds of dead bodies and of people walking around in a stupor with swollen faces and legs, their eyes looking like black holes. Then there was the smell, the terrible stench of death, of decomposed bodies, and of feces. For weeks now we had lived in filth, covered by our own feces and infested by millions of lice. This is how our liberators found us.

Now our misery was over. We survived. But not all were so lucky. Many of my friends were too weak and died within a few days of our liberation. Little joy was felt in spite of the fact that we were safe. All I could think of was my father and brother. Would I find them? Did they survive?

In Bergen-Belsen the women's camp was separated by wires from the men's camp, so we could see the condition of the men only from a distance. The scattered bodies of the dead were clearly visible. There were many more dead among the men than among the women. All the men still living looked like skeletons. I was afraid to look in their direction, afraid that my father or brother would be among the living dead. They would never recognize me, and I would not be able to tell them apart from the other prisoners. All had the same gray-looking skin, hollow eyes, swollen faces and legs. I prayed that my father and brother would not be among the men in Bergen-Belsen.

At first the British sent only medical personnel into the camp. They saw the horrible sanitary situation and quickly recognized that a typhoid epidemic was raging in the camp.

Inmates begged the liberators for food. Some of the soldiers threw boxes of biscuits over the fence. Some threw chocolate bars for the starving women. As soon as these were swallowed, those who could not control their hunger and ate despite warnings fell over and died. Our intestines had shrunk from the long period of starvation, and we were unable to digest food. Wisely, the British imposed a diet of powdered milk diluted with water. As with a baby formula, we were fed only that the first few days until we were able to eat and digest regular food.

After we adjusted to the food, the next step was the disinfection of all living ex-prisoners. The danger of spreading the dreaded typhoid was great. Ambulances drove into the camp, and one by one we entered to be disinfected by DDT. I can still see the white powder covering me from head to toe. Then began the removal of the ill to the now empty SS camp in Belsen.

Former SS barracks were converted into hospitals, and the British asked for nurses. They wanted only those who had previously had typhoid fever and were now immune. Because I had this disease in the spring of 1944, I volunteered to help with the sick.

Weighing only close to eighty pounds myself, the job of nursing the sick was taxing, not only physically but emotionally. Twelve hours a day or night I had to comfort and feed the terribly sick women. Among them were young girls. During my first week as a nurse a beautiful young Hungarian girl died in my arms. I was unable to deal with death. I knew death during the many years in camps and ghettos, but I couldn't face it now when we were supposed to live. At this point I collapsed, thus ending my career as a nurse.

We had our living quarters on the fourth floor of the hospital, and there I spent a few weeks to regain some strength. We had a radio in the room, and I can still hear the voice of Winston Churchill announcing the German surrender. The day was May 8, 1945. Everybody celebrated, but I was still too weak for any festivities.

I had been free since April 15 when the Second British Army entered Bergen-Belsen. Now three weeks later the war was over. True, I was free. But was it really over for me? I faced living with the terrible feeling of guilt because I was alive. The scars of the war I shall bear for the rest of my life.

# Chapter 17

# MEMORIES OF MY BROTHER

Each year, when January comes around, I cannot help but think of my brother. I was four years old when he was born on January 24, 1928, in Zoppot, but I can recall many details about his birth as if it were yesterday.

When my father said goodnight to me that evening, he told me that, by the time I awoke the next morning, "the stork will have delivered a brother or a sister for you." At the age of four I was a little confused. Is a brother a girl or a boy? And is a sister a boy or a girl? When I entered my parents' bedroom the following morning, I was told, "Mira, you have a little brother." The baby was in a wicker basket, and when I saw him being changed, I realized to my amazement that "a brother is a boy." My parents were so happy, especially my father. Now he had a son to carry on the family name. Until his birth, my father used to say jokingly, "My first-born son is a girl."

According to Jewish law and tradition, on the eighth day after the birth of a boy the baby has to be circumcised. This important event, called "Brit Mila" in Hebrew, was scheduled for the first day of February. This day was my father's birthday. Knowing my father's love for sweets, my Nanny took me to the Mix Chocolate store days in advance. There I bought a golden basket filled with my father's favorite bittersweet chocolates.

My parents and I and my new brother lived at Promenadenstrasse #14 in Zoppot, a suburb of Danzig. Our apartment was on the second floor. Below us lived our distant cousins, the Blochs. Their two sons, Richard and George, were also born in this building. My nanny and I went to the Blochs' apartment to stay until after the circumcision was over and a name was given to my brother. He was named Benno Benjamin after my paternal great-grandfather. Once the ceremony was over, my father came downstairs to get me. At this time I gave him the birthday gift, the basket with chocolates.

We had moved from Zoppot to Danzig when Benno was only a few months old to save my father the trouble of commuting. He wanted to spend more time with his family.

I recall the many colds Benno had, strep throat, and even stays in the hospital. He seemed always to be sick until his tonsils were removed. Many times I too wanted to be ill so that I could stay home and miss school.

From early years, Benno was always my best friend. Later he became my confidante. He was very bright and idealistic. But he was rebellious and independent too. He always tried to do exactly what he wanted.

When I joined the Zionist Youth movement, "Habonim," Benno joined "Akiba." We had endless discussions about which organization was better. We studied Hebrew with a private tutor, Mr. Glueckmann, who lived quite a distance from our home. Benno had the first hour and waited until I was finished. It was safer to walk together. By then members of the Hitler Youth were attacking Jewish children. They used sticks and rocks, and one winter day Benno came home from school with a swollen face. He had been attacked by some Hitler Youth boys, who threw rock-filled snowballs at him.

Our summers were spent at the sea resorts in Zoppot or Orlowo. How well I remember the summer of 1937. We rented an apartment for the summer months from my parents' friends in Zoppot. During the week my father stayed in Danzig and came to Zoppot for weekends. One day when Benno was nine and I was not quite fourteen, he wanted to read a novel by Alexander Dumas that I had checked out from the library. My mother told him she thought he was too young to read it, and Benno answered, "Father would let me read it." My mother responded that he should ask his father. In the meantime I continued reading while my mother went to the bedroom to rest. About four in the afternoon we noticed that Benno was not in the house. I went outside, walked to the woods where we used to go, and called out his name. But there was no sign of Benno.

My mother and I both became very worried. We were scared that something bad must had happened to him. My mother telephoned my father and told him the story about the book and that now we couldn't find him. My father said, "Maybe he really went to ask my permission to read the book and is on the way to Danzig." This sounded logical, but how could Benno walk the twenty-five kilometers from Zoppot to Danzig without telling us? My father promised to drive his car toward Zoppot. If Benno were walking toward Danzig, my father would find him.

Just minutes later, my father telephoned. He had found Benno across from the Danzig railroad station. Benno had walked from Zoppot to Danzig. He was almost home since our apartment in Danzig was five minutes away from the railroad station. I will never forget how relieved we were that Benno was safe with my father. Yes, Benno was adventurous.

Both Benno and I had dreams about going to Palestine. From Danzig, Jewish children were taken by Kindertransport to England, but he and I wanted to go to Palestine. Time was running out. War broke out, and our family was caught in Danzig. Our dreams were shattered, and there was little hope of getting out.

Next came life in the ghettos of Poland. Benno with his Aryan look could easily pass for a German. He spoke the language fluently and many times risked his life. He would remove the Jewish armband and venture outside the ghetto to bring some food for us. By January 1941 we lived in the Tomaszow Mazowiecki ghetto with my paternal grandparents. Because all schooling for Jewish children was prohibited and Benno was approaching the time of his Bar Mitzvah, he took secret Hebrew lessons from an older man. At thirteen, Benno was already six feet three inches tall; during the first two war years he had outgrown all of his clothes. When the day of his Bar

Last photograph of Mira's brother, Benno, taken January 1941 at the
Tomaszow-Mazowiecki ghetto at his Bar Mitzvah. He was killed in
April 1945 at age seventeen during the death march.

Mitzvah arrived, only my father and grandfather were able to witness his becoming "a Jewish adult." My grandfather had given Benno his old suit so that a tailor could alter it for him to wear on this special day. My grandfather was as tall as his grandson, and among the few mementos I have managed to preserve is a photograph of Benno taken in his "new" and only suit.

Food was very scarce. We had barely enough for two meals a day. Yet we wanted so much to celebrate Benno's Bar Mitzvah. The Kolski family, natives of Tomaszow, lived in the apartment above us. They had three daughters and two sons, and their youngest daughter, Eva, and I became best friends. Eva knew how much we wanted to have a special meal and told her mother about Benno. My parents were touched when Mrs. Kolski invited all of us for lunch, a simple but meaningful meal following Benno's being called to the Torah. After we ate, Benno delivered his speech, which consisted mainly of words of thanks and gratitude, but also was filled with hope for the future.

As life in the ghetto became more difficult and sometimes hopeless, Benno and I had many discussions about the outcome of the war, speculating about a future for us. Benno's views became more militant as our lives became more and more endangered. He wanted so much to fight the Nazis. He did not want to be passive.

By January 1942, my parents were struggling to get enough food to keep us from the perpetual hunger we felt. My mother was making soap to sell for bread. I was washing and ironing people's clothing. I even tutored young people in secrecy.

One memorable January evening when we returned to our room, we found a note on the table. Signed by Benno, it read: "Dear ones—I decided to escape. Be well. Chazak V'ematz. Love, Benno."

We were stunned. Speechless and petrified, we did not know what to do. Benno had no money and no Aryan papers. If anyone asked for identification, he would be killed.

Dark was approaching. The curfew would soon be in effect, and we would not be able to leave our home. Who might know about his plans? I remembered that Benno had a girlfriend named Stefcia Koniecpolska, who lived in the house bordering our back yard. I ran to see Stefcia. All she knew was that Benno was talking about joining the Polish army in Russia to fight against the Nazis. She said that Benno had a Polish friend who wanted to join the army with him.

When I returned home and told my parents about Benno's plan, they contacted a friend with the Jewish police who could walk outside the ghetto after curfew. He promised to go to the railroad station to search for Benno.

When our friend returned at almost ten that night, he told us that he found Benno and his Polish friend waiting to board a train going east. Benno was not wearing his Jewish armband. The friend brought Benno back to the ghetto. The Polish boy was handed over to the Polish police and later taken to his parents. Benno spent the night in the ghetto prison.

He never forgave my parents for apprehending him and preventing his escape. Many times, when we were already in concentration camps, I regretted that Benno was not given the chance to escape. My parents meant well. They wanted him to be safe with us in the ghetto. We did not know then what awaited us. Who knows? Benno's escape might have succeeded. He might have survived.

From then on my father made sure Benno was with him. Both worked at forced labor for the Organization Todt, named for Fritz Todt, a prominent Nazi. Because of this, both were outside the ghetto during its liquidation when my mother, grandparents, uncles, aunts, and cousins were taken to the death camp at Treblinka.

After the aborted escape, Benno became very quiet. The fire within him had died, and he was never the same again. He lost the will to fight. Benno was so thin, his resistance so low, he was among the first to come down with typhoid when we came to our first concentration camp in Blizyn. My father sold the gold bridge from his mouth to obtain some bread and butter for Benno, who recovered but seemed taller and thinner with each day.

Finally came July 1944. Our camp was to be evacuated. My father,

Benno, and I, together for the last time, were in the cattle car on the way to Auschwitz. We still hoped the Soviet army might liberate us. Completely unaware of what awaited us in Auschwitz, and trying to keep our hopes high, we agreed to meet again in Danzig once the war was over. We parted at the gate of Auschwitz-Birkenau, where I saw Benno for the last time. I waved to him as we, the women, were ordered to walk toward the camp. We never had a chance to say a proper goodbye.

Months later in January 1945 Auschwitz was evacuated. In bitter cold weather I walked the road out of Hindenburg toward Gleiwitz. On the Silesian road I saw bodies of hundreds of men shot because they were too slow or unable to walk. I was afraid to look at their faces, afraid that I might recognize my father or brother among the corpses. Since we parted, I carried their images in my heart. Now all of us looked like ghosts, our faces dark gray, our eyes lifeless. My hope was that my father and Benno were together and that, with my father's help, my brother would survive.

For me the war ended on April 15, 1945, in Bergen-Belsen. Some weeks later I was handed a piece of paper with a message in my father's handwriting. He had given copies like this to everybody who was traveling within Germany. On it was my name, the place and date of my birth, and Benno's name and place and date of birth. I was euphoric. Now I knew my father was alive and looking for his children but that he and Benno had been separated.

A few weeks later my father arrived in Belsen, where I was impatiently waiting for him. At that time I was working for the British Red Cross. Our reunion was one of the happiest moments of my life, overshadowed only by the uncertainty about Benno. We recalled the promise: to meet in Danzig after the war. Twice my father smuggled himself over the borders to get to Danzig. He did not find Benno there. Finally, my father decided to go from one concentration camp to another to search in the registers for Benno. He went to the Mauthausen Concentration Camp in Austria, where he found the name "Benno Ritschke" (the German spelling of our name) with the birth date January 24, 1927. The place of birth was listed as Zoppot. He reasoned that Benno gave his year of birth as 1927 instead of 1928 because by then my brother would have known that younger boys were sent to the gas chambers. Obviously he had made himself a year older.

The search for my brother went on for quite some time. I have a letter written to me by my father in January 1946. In it he expressed the hope still to find his eighteen-year-old son. All hopes were shattered, however, when a man who had been on the same march with Benno approached my father in Hannover. From him my father learned that by the end of April 1945, when all camps were evacuated and prisoners were marching all over Austria, Benno was too weak to continue and was shot. Just a few days later the American army liberated the surviving prisoners. For Benno it was too late. At the age of seventeen, he too had become a victim of Nazi mass murder.

I have no grave to visit. Benno's exhausted and emaciated body is buried somewhere in Austria. I will never know where. So bright, so independent, so idealistic, had he lived he could have been a valuable asset to the world. He might have achieved much to benefit mankind.

I go back many times to the years when Benno and I were carefree children. We had dreams about the future. We talked often about the Jewish homeland. Benno could have been a part of Israel; he would have been so happy there.

My father never got over the loss of his son. The evening before he died in 1979 in Tel-Aviv, he asked me, "Why did God allow me to survive? Why did Benno have to die?"

Each year on January 24, Benno's birthday, I light the memorial candle. He continues to live in my memory. His name now lives on in my eldest son, Benno, who also was born in January.

*Chapter 18*

# EVA

June 24, 1994

My Dearest Eva,

Today would be your seventy-first birthday. For the first time in more than fifty years I did not send you my very best wishes. Last year's birthday greetings came too late. You left this world before they arrived.

I remember when we met for the first time in December 1940 in your hometown of Tomaszow Mazowiecki. Jews were being herded into a ghetto. Your family and mine moved into the same building. As a well-known family who resided in Tomaszow for many generations, yours was given a five-room apartment on the second floor. We, the refugees from Danzig and Warsaw, were fortunate to be allotted one small room. Our room was just under your living room, and we were able to hear the lovely singing voice of your oldest sister, Hela, as she accompanied herself on the grand piano. How I envied you the piano. We had to leave ours behind in Danzig, and I wanted so much to play the pieces of music I had learned and loved.

Yours was a close-knit family. You had two older brothers, Moritz and Motyl, and two older sisters, Hela and Regina, as well as the kindest parents, Amsel and Leah Kolski, who showered you with their love. In comparison my family was small. I had only one brother and my dear parents. But in no time at all your parents befriended us.

I recall that a few months after we met, my brother, Benno, was approaching his Bar Mitzvah. He took secret Hebrew lessons in the ghetto because teaching and learning the language had been prohibited. On the day of his becoming a Bar Mitzvah in January 1941, your parents prepared a luncheon in your apartment for our family. My brother gave his Bar Mitzvah speech at the table. I shall never forget how moved we were by your parents' generosity, especially since food was so hard to come by.

Both of us were so young—only seventeen. Endlessly we discussed plans for the future. We kept no secrets from each other. We talked about our loves and infatuations and about the things we liked and disliked. We were as close as sisters. When I tried to persuade you to join the Zionist Youth organization Hashomer Hatzair, you had to ask your parents. They refused permission because in the ghetto belonging to any organization was forbidden. I understood. Your whole family would have suffered if you had been caught.

I never will forget the morning after the April massacre. Both of us walked the streets of the ghetto petrified by what we saw: murdered members of the Judenrat, Jewish ghetto police, and members of the Jewish intelligentsia lying in the gutters. Together we walked behind the wagon with the bodies of the dead to the gates of the ghetto, paying our last respects.

Then came the tragic day of the liquidation of our ghetto. One day before, my family left Zgorzelicka Street for Stolarska Street to stay with the families of OT workers. Both my father and brother worked at forced labor for the OT. You came to see me there. We cried and worried about the future of our families. Then we parted.

When we were reunited, just three days later, you were the only one who remained of your whole family. I was so fortunate: my father, brother, and one uncle were still with me, although no one else. As soon as we were taken to the small ghetto, "the Block," you moved in with us and we remained together. I shall never forget your despair, your nightmares, after you lost your dear ones. At that time we still did not know the whole truth. The Nazis told us that our families were taken east to work. My mother, grandparents, uncles, aunts, and cousins were among those who were shipped east. Only much later did we learn their fate in the death camp of Treblinka.

Then rumors reached us that the Block would be liquidated. We feared that we too would be sent east. You decided to leave illegally for the Polish side, with friends there offering to help you escape, but you had neither money nor the necessary papers. To live on the Aryan side required wearing nice clothes. I still had a pair of my mother's best shoes: maroon suede pumps. They fit you perfectly, and I gave them to you. Your plan was to leave our marching column before we returned to the Block from work. We spoke the whole day about your escape. You hesitated and couldn't decide what to do. Your Polish friend was to meet you, but you were scared. Finally, you decided against leaving. My feelings were mixed. On the one hand I wanted you to save yourself. On the other hand I was so afraid that you might be caught and killed.

When the Block was liquidated in May 1943, we marched together to the cattle car. With my father, brother, uncle, and you at my side, we rode locked up like cattle, destination unknown. Finally the train stopped near the Blizyn Camp, our first concentration camp. You and I moved into the same barracks, slept on the same bunk. You worked sorting clothing, I worked in the camp laundry. Both of us came down with typhoid. Both of us miraculously survived this dreaded disease.

That very little food was available in Blizyn is an understatement. The rations allotted us were too small to sustain life. We bartered every stitch of clothing we could spare. Always hungry, constantly dreaming of food, we grew weaker day by day. Another day I will never forget was when you handed me my mother's shoes, the ones I gave you to wear when you planned to escape. I did not want the shoes back, but you insisted. "You have a father and brother, and they need more food than I," you said. You could have bartered the shoes for bread for yourself, yet you gave them back to me. I have never forgotten your kindness, selflessness, and good character.

When the Blizyn Camp was to be evacuated and all of us taken to Auschwitz, we made this fateful journey together. You gave me the only photo you had of your parents and siblings to hide with my pictures, and I guarded them until we were liberated.

In Auschwitz we lived together in constant fear of selections and gassing. Sleeping on a bunk with three other girls, we tried desperately to give moral support and hope to each other. And when the day came that they selected women for slave labor in Germany's war industries, you and I left Auschwitz together for Hindenburg, a satellite camp of Auschwitz.

In Hindenburg you worked at the Tempergiesserei (foundry) while I became the camp scribe. Whenever I had extra food, I shared it with you. Now we saw each other only on Sunday afternoons. I could see how your strength was diminishing after the hard work in the foundry. Then I became very ill with typhus and had to be isolated. The next time we were together again was on the morning of the evacuation of our camp. This time we had to walk; there were no trains.

In snow and ice, you supported me during this unforgettable death march. I was so weak I could barely walk. You and other friends would not let go of me. You did not let me fall behind the column. All those who stumbled or fell behind were shot.

When we finally arrived in Gleiwitz and were loaded into open coal cars, you and I traveled together for weeks until we arrived at the Bergen-Belsen Concentration Camp. Here we were separated. I was ordered to one of the Blocks; you to another. Our friend Tobka Landau still had a gold coin that she had well hidden. She gave it to a Kapo in exchange for a job in the camp kitchen. You and Tobka shared a bunk. From then on Tobka provided you and other friends with additional food. Because of her, you and the other girls from Tomaszow and Blizyn survived this camp. Tobka was a most generous person, and I know how much you loved her and how much you suffered when she died later in Israel.

Liberation came on April 15, 1945. You decided to leave for Munich when the war was over. Your dream was to pursue a career in music, always your love.

After the war, Eva Kolska and Mira Ryczke are pictured in Belsen, a displaced persons' camp. September 1945.

I visited you in Munich a year after you left Bergen-Belsen. By this time I was married and stayed in your apartment with my husband, Max. You did not want to remain in Germany. Your dream was to continue your studies in Italy, the land of music. After you left for Italy, Max and I emigrated to the United States. You were contacted in Italy by the Jewish Brigade and left for Israel. At the kibbutz where you lived, you met Sam Horwitz, your future husband. The next time I heard from you, you and Sam had married and moved to Capetown, where his family had lived for many generations.

You had children: first Allan, then Martin, then Leora. I had the good fortune to meet all three of your children, but I never met Sam. Thousands of miles separated us, but in spite of the distance, we remained close.

Both of us were letter writers, and we shared both happy and sad moments via mail.

After more than thirty years, we met again in November 1979. You came to the unveiling of my father's grave in Israel, where you also met my two sons, Benno, named for my lost brother, and Gene, named for my mother. We saw each other again in 1984 when you came to the United States to visit your son, Allan. You came to my home in Oak Ridge, Tennessee, for two days. We talked the whole time, trying to utilize every minute of the precious time we had together.

For many years you tried to persuade me to visit you in Capetown, but my husband was ill and I could not leave him. When Max died in 1990, I wrote you that I would plan a visit to you in three or four years. First I had to return to Poland, to the place where we suffered, to the places where we lost our families. In 1991 I returned to Tomaszow and sent you a photo of the house on Zgorzelicka Street #37. You were very moved, but you wrote that you would never return to Poland. And then you wrote: "Do not wait too long. Do not delay your visit to Capetown."

The next news I heard was that you suffered a mild stroke. You continued writing to me. You were getting stronger. Then came news about the second stroke. Your daughter, Leora, wrote that you were not able to walk or talk. I began writing to you in English; always before we used Polish, but I wanted Sam to be able to read my letters to you. When I returned from my third trip to Poland in June 1993, a letter was waiting for me. Leora informed me that you had died peacefully on May 12, a month before.

I never made it to Capetown, but memories we shared of the many years together, the times in the ghetto, the camps, our terrible losses, and our lives after the war, will never leave me.

Happy Birthday, dearest friend, wherever you are.

# Chapter 19

# NEW LIFE—NEW LOVE

Free at last from the Nazi tyranny, I began to think of the future. From weighing eighty pounds at liberation, I started gaining at record speed. Always hungry, I could consume a pound of butter at one sitting. Soon the great amount of food I ate showed. I gained a few pounds every week and soon reached my normal weight and appetite.

After my disastrous experience as a nurse in the Belsen hospital, I started to work as an interpreter, first for the British Army and then for the British Red Cross. Everyone was searching for missing relatives or friends. Former concentration camp inmates traveled from one camp to another to find their dear ones. As we searched, we found many whom we had thought dead and learned the sad truth about some we hoped to find alive.

In one of the Belsen camps I found Halinka Frydlender, the daughter of my mother's cousin from Lodz. We were about the same age, and besides being relatives, we were close friends. Halinka's parents had been shot by the Nazis in Piotrkow, where the family lived during the war. Her two brothers, Paul and Rafael, escaped to Russia, and Halinka did not know whether they survived. Luise, her roommate in Belsen, was her best friend, and both of them were considering the idea of leaving Germany for Sweden, a country that was taking in Holocaust survivors. Both Halinka and Luise begged me to go with them to Sweden, but I still had high hopes that my father and brother were alive, so I did not want to leave Germany. "They will never find me if I go with you to Sweden," I told them. I was glad I did not leave because a few weeks later I got the note written by my father at the end of the war. I was so happy to know that he was alive.

I continued my work for the British Red Cross, helping families to be reunited. In December my father and I were invited to Bochum to spend Christmas with the Feldhege family. Willy Feldhege was my father's boss while he worked for the Organization Todt in Tomaszow. Mr. Feldhege sent food with my father for our family while we were in the ghetto, so thanks to him we had a little more to eat. He took that risk for us although the Nazis had forbidden anyone to help Jews. Many times he urged my father to escape to the outside while they drove the huge OT trucks. He was a most decent and kind person. I was happy that now I would have a chance to meet his wife and family.

My father was then living in Hannover, not far from Belsen. He rented a room from a German family and started to apply for a license to open the same kind of business he had in Danzig before the war. Many former Danzig acquaintances, all Germans, now lived in Luebeck, not far from Hannover, and they were most helpful to my father.

I traveled from Belsen to Hannover, and from there my father and I took a train to Bochum where the Feldheges lived. Willy and Mienchen Feldhege were a little younger than my father. They never had children, but they loved their nieces and nephews. The week I spent with them at the end of 1945 was one of the most pleasant times in my life. They showered us with gifts. They gave me fabric to have some clothes made because I had no real wardrobe at all. We remained close friends until both of them died in the late 1980s.

After the holidays, we returned home, my father to Hannover and I to Belsen. The weather was gray, damp, and cold. No snow, just a penetrating chill filled the air. I had a tiny room in the Block where I worked. A friend of mine, Aaron, who was in charge of the Block, kept my key when I was away for the holidays. He was a barber and had his shop not far from where I lived. As I entered his shop to ask for my key, Aaron was giving a haircut to a dark and handsome man. "I want you to meet an old and close friend of mine from the Piotrkow ghetto. His name is Mietek Kimmelman," he told me. People in the ghetto knew this man as Mietek, but his name was really Max.

I said hello but did not pay any real attention to the man to whom I was introduced and left for my room. This was December 27, 1945, and my friends planned to have a little party on New Year's Eve. They asked if my father could bring some drinks from Hannover. Since December 31 that year fell on a Monday, I had time to telephone my father to ask him to join us for the evening.

Aaron and his wife, Ella, were hosts for the party in their room. As soon as my father and I entered, I saw Mr. Kimmelman, the man Aaron had previously introduced to me. This time I had a chance to talk with him while we danced. He was an excellent dancer and easy to talk with. I do not remember speaking to another person the whole evening. Something drew us together. We were instantly attracted to each other. During the course of the evening Max told me that when he arrived in Belsen, he had no place to stay. Aaron took him to my room, for which he had the key, and told him that I was away and probably would not mind if he stayed in my room. Max refused. He told me he saw a picture on the chest in my room. He asked Aaron who the girl in the picture was, and was told that this was Mira, who lived in this room. "I saw your picture and knew that I had to meet you. I fell in love with the person in this picture," Max told me as were toasting the New Year 1946. So began the romance between Max and me.

This was not my first romance, however. When we lived in Gdynia in 1938, I met a young man, Bruno Chaim, and we fell in love. I was fifteen; he was nineteen. When war broke out, he was arrested and killed in 1940 in the Stutthof Concentration Camp.

During my years in the Tomaszow ghetto, at seventeen I was infatuated with the son of the owners of the apartment where we lived. He was a blond, blue-eyed young man of twenty, and we saw each other every day

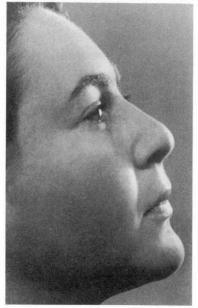

Willy Feldhege, Mira's father's German boss at Organization Todt, who helped the family with extra food, 1949.

Mira's photograph taken in Hannover, November 1945. Max Kimmelman saw the picture and fell in love with the person in it.

Max Kimmelman, when he and Mira met in December 1945.

Max's daughter by his first marriage, Maryla (Malka) Kimmelman, age two. She was killed with her mother at age eight at Treblinka.

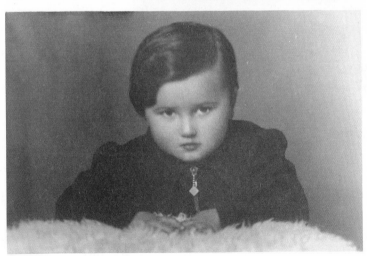

Wedding photograph of Max and Mira Ryczke Kimmelman, at Rötz-Opf,
Germany, May 1946.

when I had to walk through the room he occupied. We were not allowed to
talk with each other, meaning *he* was not allowed to talk to me. His family
was extremely orthodox. Their beliefs meant any contact between girls and
boys, men and women, was prohibited unless they were married. So how
did we communicate? At first he was always there when I had to carry the
buckets with water from the pump in the yard to our room. Somehow he
knew when I was going to fetch water and offered to carry the buckets upstairs. He stopped at the door and I had to carry the buckets the rest of the
way. That way his parents could not see that their son was helping a strange
girl. The next meetings were in the cellar where I was sent to get wood for
the stove.

Each apartment had its own cellar, and part of the Lach cellar was for our use. Moniek followed me whenever he saw me carry an empty basket. He had no problem guessing where I was going. So we spent five minutes together, stealing a kiss and a hug. What an innocent romance! We enjoyed each other's company so much that we decided to meet outdoors too. With winter on the way, we took long walks near the edge of the ghetto where there were only empty fields and not another soul around. The cold wind blew as we met every day for an hour's walk. Holding hands, we spoke about our lives before the war. What a different life each of us had. From Moniek I learned about the strict rules governing the orthodox Jews in Poland, and about his upbringing and deep respect for his parents. Whatever they said was holy. Soon I understood the strength of the orthodox family.

Someone must have seen us during one of our innocent walks and notified Moniek's parents. One week later Moniek told me that his parents had arranged a marriage for him and we would not be able to see each other again. Although he said he was completely devastated, he would do what his parents wanted. One month later he was married and moved to his wife's apartment. This was at the end of 1941. Soon his wife became pregnant and gave birth just a few weeks before the ghetto was liquidated. Moniek, his wife and son, his parents, his sister and her family were soon all sent to their deaths in Treblinka.

Most of my friends had beaus. Love gave hope to our hopeless lives. When a person had a close relationship, the word "cousin" was often used. A "cousin" could be a friend or a lover. I had many friends, but no true love. Most such friendships were platonic.

Once the ghetto was liquidated and we were sent to Blizyn, this was the end to my romances. By now starvation took all my energy, and the only thing left was the will to survive. Only the camp "elite" were able to pursue their love lives, and they did, in Blizyn as well as Auschwitz. Then came liberation.

As soon as our bodies recovered from the years of deprivation, people sought love and formed unions. Deprived for so many years of what seemed normal to young people, marriages were performed at a record pace. My first postwar romance was with the British officer for whom I was working. A wonderful and well educated Cambridge man, he and I spent hours together talking about the war, our experiences, our families, and the future. He was an observant Catholic. I was observant Jewess. We knew that what attracted us to each other was the need to have someone to be with, to talk with. We took long rides in his Jeep. The spring of 1945 was simply beautiful, ideal for excursions. Soon he was transferred to another city, but we kept writing each other. When his orders came for a transfer to India, he returned to Belsen, and we parted as friends. For months we continued to write each other. He sent me books about Jewish history or on Jewish themes. But we knew that friendship was the only thing between us. Our correspondence ended when I wrote him about my forthcoming marriage to Max.

Max asked me to marry him on January 6, just ten days after we met. It was sudden, and I did not give him an immediate answer. I felt I did not really know him at all and needed more time. At that time Max lived in the American Zone of Germany in the part known as Oberpfalz, close to Bohemia. The town in which he lived was Rötz, with a population of eight thousand. He came to this part of Germany after being liberated in Czechoslovakia and was sent to Germany because this is where he was born.

My father met Max only during the New Year's Eve party, and I felt that I should confide in him. His response was: "You will not marry a man who is more than fifteen years older than you." This was his number one objection. "You will not marry a man who was married before and lost his wife and daughter," was the second objection he gave me. "You are too young to be married. You should think about your education," was his third objection.

Of course I was thinking about my education. When Max and I met I already had a permit to go to Heidelberg to enroll at the university. I wanted to study law. All this changed suddenly. But naturally I did not want to upset my father. After all, I loved him and he was the only family I had left. Max and I discussed the problem, and Max was patient and understanding. We decided that we had to allow the idea of our marriage to sink in and to hope that my father would give in. By now I was very sure that I wanted to become Max's wife, but I had to develop a strategy so my father would see that we were both serious, that we truly wanted to be together.

Max returned to Rötz, and every day a letter arrived. In every letter he asked whether my father had changed his mind. After one month Max was back. In spite of the difficulties in postwar Germany, where traveling by train took endless days, he came to Belsen every few weeks. Max did not like to travel, so it was remarkable that he endured hardships to come to Belsen so that we could be together regularly.

In the meantime, my father set about to learn more about Max. Old Jewish custom said parents had to know all about the families into which their children married. He wrote to my only uncle who survived the war, my mother's brother, Henry Hammer, who lived in Bavaria near Regensburg. Max had many friends in this medieval town who knew his family well. One day I had a letter from Max, telling me that Henry Hammer was asking around about the Kimmelman family. Did I know about it? I had no idea and right away confronted my father. Yes, he told me. He had asked my uncle to find out what kind of a family the Kimmelmans were. If I wanted to marry Max, he said that as a father he had a right to know more about him. This became a standing joke between Max and me. We knew we were winning.

For the first Passover after the war, Uncle Henry invited my father and me to his home. Henry was my mother's youngest brother; he had lost his wife and eight-year-old son during the war. He then went outside the Warsaw ghetto and lived undercover as a Pole. His Polish name was Ludwik Turkiewicz. With his future wife, Franka, who had lost her first husband in Warsaw, he escaped the camp for Poles and went to Bohemia, where they were married and later liberated. After the war they moved to Plattling near Regensburg.

When Max heard that I would be in Plattling for Passover, he suggested that my father and I come to Rötz afterwards since it was only a two-hour drive from my uncle's home. But Uncle Henry had a better idea. Why not invite Max to spend the holidays with us? This was a brilliant idea, so a day after my father and I arrived in Plattling, Max came too.

Passover 1946 fell in the middle of April, and the weather was warm. Max and I planned our wedding. We knew that my father was coming around and would give us his blessing. We brought up the subject during the holidays. "Under one condition will you be married," my father said. "It has to be a religious ceremony, with a rabbi present." Both Max and I agreed. After the holidays we began looking for a rabbi, and found one in Regensburg. "You are the first Jewish couple since the war to ask me to marry them," said Rabbi Joseph Glatzer. Because of certain prohibitions as to dates when Jewish marriages could be performed, we decided on the closest date, May 19, a Sunday, which was also Lag B'Omer, the day when marriages were allowed to take place.

Not having much family left, we knew it would be a small wedding in the living room of the apartment Max occupied in Rötz. According to traditional Jewish law, bride and groom should refrain from eating before the wedding. For Max, fasting was still an ordeal so we planned an early morning wedding. Rabbi Glatzer came by car late Saturday evening and stayed the night at Max's place. While we sat around the table, he told us the story of his survival, a moving story that Max and I never forgot.

Joseph Glatzer graduated from the University of Lwow before the war and studied to become a rabbi. When the Germans entered Lwow in 1941, he and his family escaped with Polish papers. His family was caught and executed, but in time he came to Warsaw. During the Polish uprising in the summer of 1944, when many Poles died fighting the Nazis, Rabbi Glatzer, who had told everyone he was a Catholic priest, was asked to perform the last rites to the dying. He went up to one man and knelt down to perform the rites. The man whispered to him, "Please stop—I am a Jew. Nobody knows about it, but I want to die as a Jew." Joseph Glatzer put his mouth to the ear of the dying man and told him to repeat the "Shema" with him. This is the last prayer dying Jews say. When Rabbi Glatzer finished the story, tears ran down Max's and my cheeks and we could not talk. Later, however, we thanked the rabbi for sharing this moving story with us.

The house in which Max lived belonged to a Catholic family, so for the wedding we had to remove all the crosses and holy pictures adorning the walls of his room. The owner of the house had been a Nazi official, but his wife and daughters denied ever being Nazis. The canopy was my father's tallit (prayer shawl), and Uncle Henry was the only other relative present. We had ten adult men for the quorum and a few girlfriends there. No white dress for me. I only had one dress, and it was deep rose. No formal suit for Max since he also had only one dress-up suit. But we loved each other and were happy. The lack of a reception did not matter to us, but there was a modest brunch.

May 19, 1946, was one of the happiest days in our lives. My new life with Max began when we said our vows, when we promised each other to love, support, respect, and help each other until death would us part. We lived according to these vows for almost forty-four years.

# Chapter 20

# COMING TO THE UNITED STATES

Max and I began our married life in a small town, Rötz, in Bavaria. The population was 100 percent Catholic. No Jew had ever lived here before the war. Not far away was a town even smaller, Stamsried. In February 1945, when many camps near Bohemia were being evacuated, prisoners were brought to Stamsried, where they were liberated by the American Army in April 1945. The distance from Rötz to Stamsried was only fifteen kilometers, yet no one in Rötz had heard of concentration camps. No one ever heard of Nazi atrocities against Jews. In Rötz nobody was a Nazi. Everyone was against Hitler. This was the atmosphere in which Max and I lived. We were issued food coupons, which gave us too much to die but not enough to live on. The American Joint Distribution Committee sent food for former Jewish camp inmates to Germany. From Rötz we had to travel to Regensburg to get any of it.

By 1946 my father and I had written to friends in America and to my father's only relative, an uncle who lived in Cincinnati, Ohio, near his daughter Rose and two sons. Uncle Max was my paternal grandmother's brother, who went to America in 1905. By the time World War II ended, he was an elderly, retired man with no means to bring us to the United States. But Uncle Max helped get the necessary papers for my father and me to leave Germany. By the time the papers arrived, I was married and of course I would not leave without my husband, Max. We wrote Uncle Max about the complication. Another two years went by until all the papers arrived and we could leave for the United States.

Why didn't we go to Palestine? For years I was active in Zionist Youth movements. At first I wanted to go only to Palestine. My father reasoned, "We have nobody there. Only you and I are left. In Cincinnati, an uncle, aunt, and cousins live. At least we will be among relatives." It made sense. After I married Max, America was the only option since his dream had always been to go there. The thought of living in Palestine, a war-torn country, with danger from the Arabs and British, was unacceptable for Max. "I have seen too much, suffered enough during this war," he said. "I want our children to grow up in a country without war."

While waiting for visas, my father opened a seed business in Hannover. Many of the businessmen he dealt with were former colleagues from Danzig. He liked the business and felt at home in Hannover. But for Max and me every day we stayed in Germany was one day too many. Definite anti-Jewish feelings were apparent among the Rötz population. Yet we were ostracized and isolated from real Jewish life. A small, empty grocery store was given to us for a synagogue. Here we prayed without a Torah, without prayer shawls, with few prayer books, on our holidays. In letters to friends in America I asked for prayer shawls for my husband and father, and for prayer books.

Almost thirty former inmates from Stamsried had settled in Rötz, but it seemed that every few weeks one of our friends left. Some went to Palestine, others to South America. Two other families waited for U.S. visas. In the meantime Max became president of the small Jewish community and I served as secretary. Tutoring in English kept me busy because everyone wanted to learn the language.

While anxiously waiting to leave Germany, we made contact with Max's sister-in-law, who was German. She and Max's older brother,

From left: Max, Mira, and Mira's father, Moritz Ryczke. Rötz-Opf, Germany, November 1946.

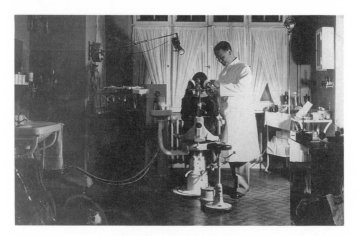

Max's brother, Michael Kimmelman, in his dentist's office in Berlin, 1927. He survived the war using Polish identity papers.

Mira's school friend, Tula, from the Polish Gimnasium in Danzig. Gdynia, 1938.

Mira's sponsoring Cincinnati family, 1948. From left, standing: Faith Roth, Mira, Rose Jacobs Roth, Sam Roth. Seated: Aunt Yetta Jacobs and Uncle Max Jacobs (brother of Mira's paternal grandmother).

Mira and her father in New York City, May 1950.

Gene and Benno
Kimmelman, Mira and
Max's sons, at their
Grandfather Ryczke's New
Jersey chicken farm, 1957.

Max Kimmelman and his
best friend, Nathan
Laznowski, from
Buchenwald Concentration
Camp, shortly after
liberation. Bohemia, June
1945.

Benno Kimmelman with "Uncle"
Nathan Laznowski, Cincinnati, April
1954.

Gene Kimmelman with "Uncle"
Nathan, and his father, Max.
Cincinnati, May 1957.

Max and Mira. Jerusalem, August
1982.

Joy and Benno Kimmelman before
their marriage, 1985.

Max and Mira celebrating forty
years of marriage, Oak Ridge, 1986.

Michael, were married in Berlin in 1925 and had two children, Peter and Vera. When Michael was expelled from Germany, his family joined him in the city of Piotrkow, Poland. After the ghetto was formed, the German wife and children were allowed to live outside the ghetto. Later they were advised by the Gestapo to leave Poland and return to Germany. Michael was helped by a good friend to escape the ghetto and lived with Polish papers until the Soviets entered Warsaw. Max enjoyed seeing his sister-in-law and her children. They visited us often in Rötz until we left for America. The contact was broken a few years later when Michael divorced his first wife and married the friend who saved his life. Michael, his wife Eva, and her daughter, Elizabeth, left Poland for Israel and lived there for many years. From there they emigrated to Canada, and we saw them many times. Michael died in July 1974 in Toronto.

The day of our departure for America arrived. My father came to Munich to bid us goodbye. He remained in Germany for one more year but was not happy there after we left.

From Munich we traveled with many refugees to Bremen. Max and I did not travel alone. We volunteered to chaperon twenty children, ten boys and ten girls. These were either Jewish orphans or children of German origin who had relatives in the United States.

With the children we boarded the army transport ship Marine Flasher and sailed first to Halifax, Canada, and then to New York City in July 1948. Our ten days on the ship were filled with ambivalence. What would we do in America? What kind of life awaited us? Would our family accept us? Endless questions, but no answers. We wanted this voyage to last because we were afraid of the unknown future. Once we saw the Statue of Liberty, however, hope and optimism entered our souls.

My father's friends from Danzig were waiting at the pier with flowers and boxes of candies. The Weiners were old friends and had known me when I was a little girl. They made us feel welcome. We spent one week in a fourth-grade hotel off Broadway, a week to explore New York City. The noise, the voices of this pulsating city, revitalized us. We loved New

York. I even met a former classmate and best friend, Tula, from the Polish Gimnasium. Her husband was a Polish attaché in New York, and we spent two days together. In Danzig she had been forbidden to talk to me, to sit next to me because I was Jewish, she a Catholic. Now it didn't matter. Suddenly she and her husband were recalled to Poland, and I never saw or heard from her again.

But Cincinnati was our destination, and we arrived at Union Station there on August 2, 1948. Uncle Max looked so much like my Grandmother Esther, it was startling. This kind man and his wife, Yetta, lived with their daughter, Rose, and her husband, Sam. They gave us the solarium to sleep in until we could find a place of our own. We had arrived with twenty-five dollars between us, money given to us for chaperoning the twenty children to America. We were poor, but we felt rich now that we were with family.

Within two days both of us found jobs: Max with the Adler Company, makers of the famous Adler socks, and I as a clerk in a bookkeeping office. We started work a week later and rented our first apartment, a furnished bedroom with a broken bed, a chair with only three legs, a small kitchen, and a bathroom.

From the beginning we decided to save a few dollars each week. I refused to purchase clothing, not even a pair of nylons, for one solid year. My cousin, Rose, sewed a cotton dress for me when she saw the heavy European dresses I wore. The summer temperature in Cincinnati was above 100 degrees, and our woolen attire was completely unsuitable. When the Jewish agency heard about us, they came to our apartment on Rockdale Avenue to offer us money for the holidays. Both of us flatly refused but thanked them for their good intentions. We never accepted one cent from any agency. We wanted to make it without charity because we were able to work.

Every Saturday afternoon we went to visit Uncle Max and his wife. This became a routine in our busy lives. Max worked sixty hours a week at hard physical labor. He did not speak English yet and was put at the hardest tasks, lifting, pushing, and carrying three hundred pounds of wool or cotton. He had never worked so hard in his life. Many times, when his spirit was low, he said, "Let's return to Germany." These low moments passed, however, and we tried to look on the brighter side of life.

A few disappointments followed. We were told in no uncertain terms: "Do not talk about your war experiences. Nobody wants to hear it." So we kept silent for twenty years. When I worked in an office with no air conditioning in summers, I had to wear short sleeves. To my anguish I was told to cover the concentration camp number up with a band-aid. "I do not want people to see it. They may think you were in prison," my boss said. After six weeks of continuous removal of band-aids, I had sores on my left arm. It was time to change jobs. Until a month before our first child was born, I worked as a clerk for the Union of American Hebrew Congregations in Cincinnati.

Thirteen months after we came to America, my father arrived. I went to New York to greet him. Mr. Weiner, our friend from Danzig, invited him to share his apartment. Weeks later my father arrived in Cincinnati and met the uncle he never saw before along with his aunt and cousins. While Max was working so many hours overtime, I took night classes at the University of Cincinnati in bookkeeping. Max had no time to learn English. When an elderly retired teacher, Miss Rosenthal, heard about his problem, she became the angel who volunteered to teach him on Sundays. My father, on the other hand, could read and write English but did not speak the language. Cincinnati was not for him. All his old friends from Danzig lived in New York. To them he could speak German, Polish, or Russian.

During the summer of 1950, my father went to the Catskills, where he met his second wife, Bella. He was very much in love with her, and we were happy he had found someone to share his life. She came to Cincinnati for the Brit Mila of our first son, Benno. A few weeks later she and my father were married. Without speaking English, it was impossible for my father to start a business in New York. Meanwhile my only surviving uncle from Plattling, Uncle Henry Hammer, came to America and settled on a chicken farm in Vineland, New Jersey. If it was a good place for my uncle, my father thought it would be good for him too. He and Bella went to live on a chicken farm in Estell Manor, not far from Vineland. "Chickens understand my language. To them I don't have to speak English," my father would say.

The most exhilarating moment in Max's and my life was the birth of our first son, named Benno after my brother. His Hebrew name was for Max's oldest brother, the one killed at Treblinka. Our lives revolved around our child. He was God's gift to us. So many of my friends were unable to have children, I felt so lucky, so blessed. Max was promoted to clerk. Later he was made foreman of a department and finally supervisor. Four years after Benno, we were blessed again with another son. He was named Gene for my mother, Eugenia, but his Hebrew names were for Max's father and my paternal grandfather. We had a wealth of names. So many of our dear ones were gone, and we wanted to keep their memories alive by giving their names to our children.

School years followed. Both boys attended public and Hebrew School. Until now we lived in furnished apartments, but we had saved enough to buy furniture. The next step was the purchase of a used car. Both Max and I took driving lessons, and soon we were able to take our children on rides and Max could drive to work. The car was a shiny green Oldsmobile, only five years old, but it turned out to be a real lemon. The expenses to fix this car far exceeded the price of a new car. We resolved from this experience never again to buy a used car.

Eventually the German government began to pay restitution to former concentration camp prisoners. Together Max and I received the sum of $4,000 in 1955, which became the down payment for the small house in Golf Manor. In 1956 we moved to 6422 Stover Avenue. We had two healthy children. Max had a good job. We lived in our own house. Life was good to us, and we felt quite fortunate.

The time soon came for our Benno to begin his Bar Mitzvah preparations. On February 15, 1964, we celebrated this important event, our first and last big celebration in Cincinnati. Two months later Max was transferred to Rockwood, Tennessee. The Adler Company sold out to Burlington Industries, and their production was moved to Tennessee.

At first I refused to move. Max traveled to Rockwood by car and came home only on weekends. This became impractical, and we missed him very much. But Rockwood had only one Jewish family, an assimilated one, and there was no synagogue or religious school for the boys. After many debates, I wrote to the nearest city with a Jewish congregation, Oak Ridge, Tennessee. Located only thirty-eight miles from Rockwood, Max agreed that if we moved there, he would commute. With this compromise, the Kimmelmans moved to Oak Ridge in August 1964.

The boys adjusted to new schools, made new friends. Our lives changed completely. Oak Ridge, being a friendly community, felt like home immediately. New friends became our extended family. One month after we arrived I began teaching in the religious school at Beth El Center. The children I taught became a vital part of me. Promoting and teaching Jewish history and culture along with the Hebrew language became my goal, my life. Involvement in Jewish and civic causes, especially Hadassah, filled the time, and I soon forgot that we ever lived in Cincinnati. No more did we have to hide the past.

Soon I was asked to share our war experiences with school children, with churches, with civic groups. While the children were still in school I became involved in their Parent-Teacher Association and their other activities. Once they left Oak Ridge for college I became even busier, spending my time and energy working as a volunteer for Hadassah, Sisterhood, Jewish Congregation, American Field Service, and the United Nations Committee.

After nineteen years of marriage, my father and Bella were divorced. "Papa," as we all called him, moved to Oak Ridge to be with us after the shock of being left by his wife. A year later he decided to go to Israel, to learn the language and to settle down there. At the age of seventy-five he enrolled in the Ulpan (Hebrew language school) for two semesters, where he made many friends. He loved the country, the people, and was happy there. On his visits to Oak Ridge he told us the wonders of the Jewish state but also gave sharp critiques about the bureaucracy. He died in my arms on March 13, 1979, while Max and I were visiting him in Israel, the land he loved so much.

How can I best describe my father? He was a complex person. My children would answer the question with a short answer: "He was a character." Extremely intelligent, opinionated, yet with a strong sense of fairness, Papa was a born optimist. He saw the world through rose-colored glasses and believed it to be good. He trusted people, who often took advantage of him. He helped everyone who came to him for money and was seldom repaid for what he gave. Charitable to all in need, he taught us to be giving too. Stubborn when it came to his own children, Papa was the one who disciplined us.

He loved the "good life," which he considered to be good cognac, chocolate, beautiful women, and fast cars. Once he learned to drive a car, Papa had more tickets for speeding than can be imagined. Yet he never had an accident because he was an excellent driver.

But of all things he loved his family best. He was a devoted husband and father and always our protector. We felt secure when he was around. We believed in his judgment and were devastated when it proved to be wrong. Had we listened to my mother's realistic thinking, we would have left Danzig before the war caught us. Papa's stubbornness, his optimism, kept us from going.

During the war years Papa tried everything he could to keep us safe, but he soon realized that matters were out of his control. When his parents and wife were taken from him, he tried desperately to protect us. Just having him near gave me a feeling of security, but it was false security. Once we arrived in Auschwitz, I was on my own. My only hope was that Papa and my brother, Benno, would stay together. This was not to be, either. While Papa was at work, the SS needed laborers and took away my brother and other young Jewish men to Mauthausen. From there Benno was sent to the satellite camp in Amstetten near Linz. There he did hard labor building and repairing railroad tracks for the German army. During the months in

Auschwitz, Papa tried to get extra food for Benno, who was weakened from the typhoid fever he suffered in Blizyn-Majdanek. He needed nourishment he could not get in Auschwitz. Once sent to the Mauthausen camp, his physical condition deteriorated further. Too weak to march in April 1945 just before liberation, Benno was shot to death. Had he remained in Auschwitz, Papa would have done anything to keep him alive.

Another example of my father's charitable conduct: While my older son, Benno, had a grant to study in Europe, my school friend, Janka Krakowska Waril from Danzig, took him into her Stockholm home. She told him, "Benno, there is a man here who knew your grandfather. When he found out that I came from Danzig, he told me that during the death march from the Kaufering Camp, a Mr. Ryczke from Danzig saved his life. Call him up and talk to him." Benno was intrigued and telephoned the man. His name was Joseph Bornstein, and he must have been the age of my brother at the time of the death march. He told Benno that my father carried him on his back when he was unable to walk. Bornstein told my son that without my father's help he would have been shot during the evacuation because he was too weak to make the long march on his own.

Papa had never mentioned this incident. When my son wrote home about it, Max and I asked him about it. He remembered the incident well and told us that all he could think of was his Benno and that he had prayed that somewhere, someone would help his son in the same way he was helping this young man. Helping others was characteristic of my father.

But he was a perfectionist and always demanding of us. When my older son studied German in college, Papa asked him to write to him in the language. Benno wrote a lengthy letter, proud that he could please Papa. A week later he got the letter back filled with corrections. This was the first and last letter Benno wrote to him in German. He was terribly hurt that Papa corrected his mistakes instead of praising him for the effort. Papa did not do it in malice, of course. He wanted Benno to learn correct German and demanded perfection.

Both of my sons loved and admired him, however, and he saw in them the son he lost. His grandsons were his world, but his ideas of discipline and

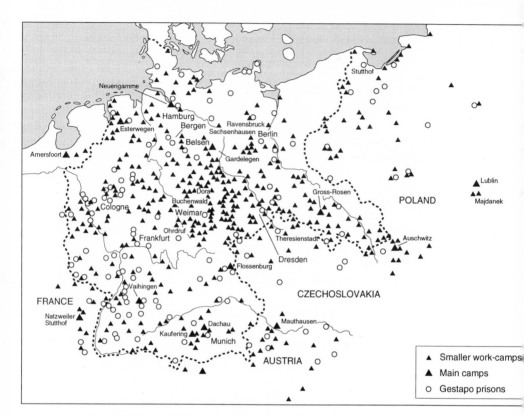

Germany, Austria, Czechoslovakia, and Poland, with death, labor, and
concentration camps indicated by dots.

teaching were not for my sons' generation and not for the United States. He could not raise them the way my brother and I had been raised, and Papa did not like facing that. But he loved life, was a good storyteller, and had stories and jokes for every occasion. He became the center of attention whenever we had company. Yes, he was a character.

The friendships that I formed in the camps were often as strong as blood relations, and Max had this experience too. During his months in the Schlieben Concentration Camp, part of Buchenwald, he met an elderly man, Nathan Laznowski. They were together until liberation, and Uncle Nathan, as we all came to call him, saved Max's life shortly before the war ended. Sick and weakened by constant diarrhea, Max fainted as he got up one morning. Nathan revived him, gave him some of the black liquid called coffee, and cared for him, something Max never forgot.

I think Max found a father figure in Nathan. Once they were liberated in Nixdorf, Nathan lost all desire to go on. "I have no one," he said, and contemplated suicide. When Max saw how depressed his friend was, he told Nathan, "You will be my uncle. Wherever I go, you will go with me." So Uncle Nathan followed Max to Germany and then to the United States. He came two years after we arrived, but not to Cincinnati. Uncle lived in Kentucky and for every holiday he came to stay with us. Our sons knew him as their uncle too, a dear and respected relative.

When we planned our move to Oak Ridge, Uncle Nathan told us that he too would move to be close to us. He joined us in 1967. Uncle had a wonderful sense of humor, a keen and sharp mind, though little formal education. Nathan was a religious and observant person, and the synagogue became the center of his life, loved and respected by the people he contacted. Eventually he was diagnosed with cancer and was in and out of the hospital. Operation followed operation, yet he did not lose hope. When doctors could do no more, we took Uncle Nathan into our home. There he died peacefully surrounded by Max, our son Benno, and me.

Uncle had become an integral part of our lives. The stories he told our sons still remember. The jokes he told are being retold. Except for Max, Uncle survived the Holocaust alone having lost his wife and two children in

Poland. He asked me to promise to care for his grave and to say the Kaddish prayer for him. Max and I went regularly to his grave. Now Max is buried next to his friend and Uncle; I continue the visits.

Max retired after twenty-five years of devoted work for Burlington Industries. For the first time we spent our time together. Max often said, "The best times were after I retired." The boys were grown; Benno married in 1975. Ups and downs did not spare us, of course. Five years after Benno married Lisa, they were divorced, a shock to Max and me.

Then Max's health began to fail. First there was a bypass on his left leg. Then his heart arrhythmia gave him trouble. A few years later he suffered kidney failure. He was a fighter and never gave up. Despite the health problems we tried to live active and productive lives. He served on the board of directors of the Jewish Congregation for eight years. He babysat for our friends' children. He sold detergent products. And we traveled seven times to Israel, twice to England, and once to Sweden. This kept him going.

In 1985 when Benno met Joy, we were elated. They were married one year later. Their wedding was the last happy occasion when Max and I could still dance. Our first grandchild, Melanie, was born April 3, 1988. Euphoric, Max and I flew to New York to celebrate her naming. She was given not only Max's mother's Hebrew name, Malka, but it was also the name of his eight-year-old daughter who perished in the Treblinka death camp in 1942. Max had adored his little girl, so the naming of his granddaughter was an extremely emotional event for him.

This was the last trip to New York we made together. From the Knoxville airport I rushed Max to the hospital, where he was prepared for dialysis. For almost two years, three times a week, Max spent hours in the dialysis clinic. His quality of life became less and less desirable, but we endured. In spite of progressively deteriorating health, Max never lost his sense of humor, nor his love for life.

Soon other problems developed. Sores on his legs caused by lack of circulation became so painful that Max had a hard time walking. First came a cane, then a walker, and finally a wheelchair. The only way he could be kept alive was to have both legs amputated. Laser treatments were tried to avoid such a drastic step, but to no avail. Finally, we sat in the hospital and tried to think reasonably. "I want to live," Max said, "even without legs." As painful as the decision was to make, it was his. The amputation took place on September 27, 1989. The recovery was slow. I had to take Max to a nursing home, and I moved in with him. From the time he first entered the hospital for the operation I never went home except to shower and change clothes. For four months Max struggled to adjust to his new condition.

By the end of January 1990 the doctor told me I could take Max home. I had to learn to lift him from his bed to a chair; from the chair to his wheelchair. Max and I joked about my operation of the lift. We tried to minimize the hopelessness of his situation. He was home. I could cook his favorite dishes and take better care of him. But all this didn't last long. On Saturday, February 10, while I was talking with Joy about their planned visit to see Max, I heard a rattling noise coming from his chest. He was having difficulties breathing. As if through a dense fog I recall dialing 911, rushing him to the hospital, nearly losing him to cardiac arrest in the ambulance. It was a nightmare. I called my children. Gene, Benno, and Joy arrived the following morning with Melanie.

Max was in the Intensive Care Unit alive and alert. He had no recollection of what had happened the day before. Jokingly he told Benno and Gene, "The doctors thought I was kicking the bucket, but I am not ready to die." He did die fifteen days later on February 25, 1990. No pain can compare with the pain of losing Max. Half of me died with him. I had to gather all my inner strength to overcome the loss. With the help of my children, my friends, and the memories of our forty-four years together, I survived again.

*Chapter 21*

# CLOSING THE CIRCLE

In my opinion the only way to teach the Holocaust effectively is to go to the places where the atrocities were perpetrated. "You have to see the places, travel the distances, talk to the people. This is the only way to understand the geography, the history of countries where the Holocaust took place," I've told many groups. I've stressed the importance of geography because many Americans do not realize how short the distances are between European cities, or how close the concentration camps were to large populations that claimed not to know they were there.

Following an October 1987 seminar retreat sponsored by the national and international organization Facing History and Ourselves, founded in Boston more than a decade ago, participants asked me, "Would you come with us? Would you translate for us?"

At that time Max was not well. His kidneys were failing, and we anticipated that sooner or later he would have to be on dialysis. Max and I had often talked about the possibility of returning to Germany and Poland. "I will never go back as long as I live," Max insisted. I wanted so much for him to visit my hometown, Danzig. I wanted to share with him the places where I grew up, show him the beauty of the city. "After I die you will be able to go back," he said.

One month after Max died, a friend from the Facing History seminar wrote me that a trip to Poland, Czechoslovakia, and Germany was being planned. My words from 1987 took roots, and in the summer of 1990 the group planned to visit the former Warsaw ghetto, Treblinka, Auschwitz, Terezin, Sachsenhausen, and Berlin. Two of the seminar participants, Jinx Bohstedt and Martha Deaderick, both Tennessee teachers, came to see me to try to talk me into going with them. "You will not be alone. We will be with you," they said. This was a time when I was in deep mourning and incapable of making any plans. I told them to give me a little more time, but because there was room for only thirty-six on the trip, they advised me to reserve a place, which I did.

I received more information in June, with the itinerary. My eyes fell on the name "Piotrkow" as I looked over the places the travelers would visit. "They will go to the city where Max's family once lived, where his parents are buried," I thought. "Yes, I will go," this helped me decide. The pilgrimage would serve my most important needs: to go to the places where my dear mother, grandparents, and most of my family perished. I could mourn at the places of their deaths. I could revisit the camp where I saw my brother for the last time. But most of all I wanted to do it for Max. I wanted to see the city where his family lived, the place where his first wife and small daughter were torn away from him.

Preparations for the journey kept me busy. In Warsaw I contacted the son of the Pole who harbored Max's sister, Helen, for more than two years. Stefan Pruc saved her life by hiding her in his home. Both Helen and Stefan died in the 1960s, but Stefan's son, Jozio, resided with his wife and son in Warsaw. Although we had never met, I knew them from letters we exchanged through the years. Now for the first time we would meet. To me Jozio was family. Helen had raised him, and he adored her.

Stefan Pruc, who saved the life of Max's sister, Helen. Krosno, Poland, 1955.

Jozio Pruc and his wife, Krystyna. Jozio is Stefan Pruc's son. Warsaw, August 1990.

Grave of Helen
Kimmelman Pruc and her
husband, Stefan Pruc,
Krosno, Poland, 1990.

Rails leading to Treblinka death camp. 1993.

Mass grave at Treblinka death camp. Only ashes and fragments of bone remained. 1990.

Mira lighting the memorial candle at Treblinka in front of the Tomaszow-Mazowiecki stone. 1990.

Some of the seventeen thousand broken stones at Treblinka, each representing a destroyed Jewish community in Europe.

Above: Piotrkow-Trybunalski, Max's family home on Starowarszawska Street 7 during and after World War I, 1991.

The picture of the Ten Commandments found on the wall of the former Great Synagogue of Piotrkow-Trybunalski during postwar renovation. Today it is a public library. August 1990.

Max's oldest brother, Yechiel Kimmelman (1888–1908),
photograph taken after his arrest in 1905 for the killing of a
Czarist policeman. He was sentenced to lifelong hard work in
Siberia, where he died two years later.

Left: Max's older brother, Leon Kimmelman, at twelve, with a friend in Piotrkow, 1910. Leon was killed with his wife, Gucia, at Treblinka in 1942.

Monument to the fallen members of the "Bund" (Jewish socialist movement) in the Piotrkow-Trybunalski Jewish cemetery. Among the names: Leon Kimmelman and wife, 1990.

I gave him all the details about my plans to visit Poland and told him to meet me at the Forum Hotel on July 24.

Jinx, Martha, and I flew to Boston; from there via London on British Airways we arrived in Warsaw. The airport at Okiecie was a dilapidated old shack with the most primitive facilities. When we arrived at the hotel in the center of the city, I could hardly recognize the place. The Warsaw I knew did not exist. Most of the houses I remembered were destroyed. New tall box-like cement buildings replaced them. In the lobby of the hotel groups from all over Europe could be heard chatting in Italian, German, and English. Poland had become a Mecca for tourists. Jozio was not to be seen, but while our group was eating supper in a separate dining room, a stout man with a bouquet of flowers entered. I immediately recognized Jozio from pictures I had seen. We fell into each other's arms, kissing and hugging each other. We talked for hours in my room. He told me about the years during the war when Helen was hidden in a cupboard. Jozio was only nine years old then, but he remembered it all. We saw each other again during our stay. I met his wife, Krysia, and son, Czarek, with his wife, Monika. They too became like family for me.

The trip to Treblinka was so emotional, so traumatic, I could barely speak. Looking for the broken stone of the city, Tomaszow, lighting the memorial candle for my dear ones at the site of the Piotrkow stone, walking among the seventeen thousand broken stones, each representing a Jewish community destroyed by the Nazis. The vastness and stillness of this place of mourning allowed me to say my prayers for all those Max and I had lost. This was their cemetery, a place where I could mourn and pray. Deep in my heart I promised myself that some day I would return here with my children. This time I had to do it alone. I needed the solitude. Although I was with a group of kind and understanding friends, I had to face the past by myself.

The next stop was Piotrkow. This city was included on the trip because one of the participants grew up there and wanted to revisit the city as I wanted to revisit Danzig. I had never been here, but I remembered the names of the streets as Max described them. Piotrkow had sixty thousand inhabitants before the war, half of them Jewish. While many in our group went to see the archives, I went to find the street and house where Max's parents and siblings once lived—Starowarszawska Street #7. As I stood in front of this house I had to think of the many times Max walked on these cobbled stones, the times when he and his brothers and sisters played here.

The next stop was the Jewish cemetery, where a group of Poles with wreaths awaited us. The flowers were placed on the grave of fifty Jewish victims shot by the Nazis. The parents of my cousin, Halinka Frydlender, were among them. I tried to locate the graves of Max's parents, but the cemetery was old, the stones broken or leaning and ready to fall. Weeds were knee deep, tombstones covered with moss, the writing on them illegible.

As we walked through the cemetery, we came upon a monument to the murdered Jewish Bund members. The Jewish Bund was an anti-Czarist Jewish workers group. Both of Max's older brothers had been active in the Bund. The oldest, Yechiel, took part in the assassination of a Czarist officer. He was sentenced to die, but Max's mother wrote a letter to the wife of the Czar and the sentence was changed to lifelong imprisonment in Siberia. This was in 1906. Two years later Max was born, and that same year Yechiel died in Siberia. After their son was arrested, Max's parents moved to Germany, where part of the Kimmelman family resided, but they returned to Piotrkow years later. Max's next-to-oldest brother, Leon, his favorite brother, after whose Jewish name (Leib-Benjamin) Benno is named, was active in the Bund most of his life. When the Gestapo arrested Bund members in 1941, he was helped to escape. With his wife, Gucia, he came to Warsaw, and both were killed in Treblinka in 1942.

I looked at this impressive monument. While reading the names my heart stopped for a second: Kimmelman Leon and Wife—these words, these names, were chiseled on the marble. Neither I nor Max knew there was a monument where his brother and sister-in-law were named. Providence must have brought me to this place.

The journey took us to Czestochowa and to the Monastery of the Black Madonna. From there we left for Cracow, and the next stop: Auschwitz. I walked through the gates of this infamous camp in a daze.

We saw all that was left to be seen. As we entered Birkenau, with only a few barracks left, I saw the place where my group had been led to the bath houses. As we got closer to the railroad tracks near the crematorium, I could see lush greenery all around us, blue sky above us, and we were breathing clean, fresh air. When I arrived in 1944 there was no grass, no trees, the air was filled with the stench of burning bodies, the sky dark from the smoke coming out of the crematoria chimneys. The Auschwitz and Birkenau I saw during this visit was not the one I saw in my heart. I could still smell and see the "other" one. I shared memories with my group, especially the moments of our arrival here, and the parting from my father and brother. I do not know whether I would have the inner strength to return here with my children. Someday they may want to make this journey without me.

Terezin was a different experience for me since I was seeing it for the first time. But I had read and lectured about it to students. Then came Sachsenhausen. My father was sent here late in 1944 after my brother was taken from Auschwitz to Mauthausen. After that there was no reason for my father to remain in Auschwitz, and he volunteered to leave with the next group. Sachsenhausen was one of the first concentration camps, and here he worked very hard before being sent to Dachau.

Our memorable trip ended in Berlin. We visited the Wannsee Villa, where the Final Solution for the Jewish people had been planned. We visited places where courageous Germans fought against Hitler. All this somehow closed the circle for me. Although emotionally I was completely drained, I never regretted making this pilgrimage. My only regret was that I had no chance to revisit Danzig, my hometown. Upon my return to the United States I shared my impressions with my children. My son Gene sensed how I longed to see Danzig. He and his future wife, Caroline, made plans for the three of us to travel there.

One year later, as the three of us arrived in Warsaw, Jozio was waiting at the airport. This time he had a chance to meet part of my family. He insisted on driving us to Danzig, and to be our driver for the week we planned to stay in Poland. After seeing the former Warsaw ghetto, the old city of Warsaw, we went to Piotrkow. Here I could be the guide for my children to show them what I saw one year ago. The city of Tomaszow Mazowiecki was only a half-hour away. We stopped here so I could point out the house we lived in at Zgorzelicka Street #37. With my children I wanted to walk the street I had walked with my dear mother for the last time and stop where the little church stood. Here was where she and I parted. Now there is a large modern church on the same spot. As we walked through the streets of the former ghetto, I told the children about my life here.

The following day we drove to Danzig. I still could not believe that I would see the city of my childhood, the city I dreamed about all these years. The drive took about six hours, and it was dusk when suddenly the skyline of Danzig was before my eyes. The last time I saw it was October 1939 when, with my family, I was forced to leave. Now it was August 1991. More than one lifetime had gone by, yet for me this city had not changed. The rooftops, the steeples of St. Mary's Church, of City Hall, St. Trinity Church were all as I remembered them despite the destruction the city had been through during World War II. Every corner, every street, yes, every stone was familiar. Facades of the old buildings hid the new and modern buildings constructed behind them, so the city was restored to its glory.

Most of the streets had been rebuilt after the Soviet army demolished much of the city in March 1945. But the streets were the same again. Only the people were gone. Not a sign was left to indicate that once upon a time more than ten thousand Jews had lived here, had helped make the city prosperous.

My task now was to introduce Danzig to my children, to make them see the city through my eyes. After checking in at the Hevelius Hotel, I took Gene and Caroline for an evening walk through the old city. Although it was dark, the streets were well lit, making it feel like "my" Danzig. Walking through them I relived my childhood and the happy memories of my early years here, which I shared with my children. Pointing here and there, telling them which of our friends lived on this street or in that building, made it come alive again for me. The next day was devoted to retracing the places where I lived with my family. We started with the twenty-minute drive to Zoppot, the sea resort where my brother and I were born. Street names were

Rails leading to the gate of
Auschwitz. August 1990.

Barbed wire and gate at Auschwitz-
Birkenau. 1990.

Destroyed cremato-
rium and gas chamber
at Auschwitz-
Birkenau. 1990.

Watch tower and old
barrack at Auschwitz-
Birkenau. 1990.

Old barrack at Auschwitz-Birkenau.
1990.

Crematorium ovens at Auschwitz I.
1990.

Mira's son Gene with his wife, Caroline. 1992.

The gate to the house on Zgorzelicka Street 37 in Tomaszow-Mazowiecki, the former ghetto where Mira and her family resided from 1940 to 1942. Photograph taken in 1991.

The building where
Mira and her family
spent their last
night together, in
October 1942.
Photograph taken in
1991.

Railroad station in
Gdansk (formerly
Danzig), Poland.
Photograph taken in
1993.

The house where Mira and her brother were born in Sopot (formerly Zoppot), Poland. Photograph taken in 1993.

Building on Swietojanska Street 66 in Gdynia, Poland, where Mira and her family lived in 1938. Arrow points to the family's apartment on the fourth floor. Photograph taken in 1991.

Max's mother, Malka
Weinberg Kimmelman, in
1920.

Max's mother's tombstone at
the Jewish Cemetery in
Piotrkow. She died at age fifty-
eight on April 17, 1925.
Photograph taken in June 1993.

all in Polish, but I did not need names. How well I remembered Promenadenstrasse #14, where I lived until I was four and a half years old. I led
Gene and Caroline to the street, to the house. Jozio could not believe that I
still remembered the place, that I could guide him. We walked the one-kilo-
meter-long Zoppot pier. To my dismay the once clear Bay of Danzig—the
Baltic Sea—was now so polluted that wading and swimming in its water was prohibited. Swans in droves swam here now, polluting the water even more.

From Zoppot we drove to the resort village of Orlowo, once a fash-
ionable place but now neglected and lifeless. I showed the children and
Jozio the houses where I spent the summer months in 1933, 1934, and 1935
with my family. Although everything else had changed, these houses had
not. Orlowo had no life left. It was now the bedroom community for the
large port city of Gdynia. Only a handful of elderly Poles were to be seen
walking or driving here.

We stopped in Gdynia at Swietojanska Street #66, the house
where we lived, and next door at #68 where our distant cousins the
Blochs from Danzig resided until their departure for Ireland in 1939. The
Ebins lived on the other side of the building at #64. Gala Ebin was my
best school friend in 1938 when we shared the same bench in the Polish
Gimnasium. While her sister, Ima, was matriculating in Warsaw, Gala and I
shared many adolescent experiences.

The Ebin family left Gdynia the week before war was declared. Both
girls—Ima and Gala—had ball gowns made to order for the voyage across
the ocean. The family left in time and did not experience the horrors of war.
Unfortunately none of the family is left, however. The parents died quite
young. Ima died of cancer at the age of thirty-two and Gala of the same disease at age fifty.

After a full day of visiting places of my youth, we returned to Danzig.
The next day we walked the streets I walked to school, to my Hebrew lessons,
to the Zionist Youth organization. We found the house on Brotbaenkengasse,
beautifully rebuilt in its old patrician style. The houses on Dominikswall
were all gone, replaced by new buildings. Yet I could recognize the spot

where our house once stood. Then we walked to the Polish Gimnasium, past the famous Trinity Church, an old, red brick building that had not changed at all. Again many memories of my years here came back. I wondered what had happened to all my teachers, the good ones and the ones who gave me trouble. Where did all the students go? Were they still in Danzig and vicinity? I had no one to answer my questions.

Our plans were to travel by ferry to Sweden and from there to Denmark. Then an unfortunate event happened: someone stole my passport while I was buying gifts to take home. It seemed ironic that fifty years ago my passport was destroyed by fire in Warsaw and now someone had stolen it. We had to go through an unbelievable amount of red tape to be able to leave for Sweden the following day: report the loss to the police; have them issue a statement about the theft; check out at the hotel; catch a train to Warsaw; get the Polish embassy in Warsaw to request a new passport. My son Gene had to swear that I had a valid passport; fortunately we had the number. Then catch the train back to Danzig to make it in time for the ferry—with twenty minutes to spare.

We made it to Sweden, but with Caroline seasick during the crossing. From there we went to Denmark to meet the family Gene had stayed with during his high-school American Field Service year abroad. His Danish family and friends welcomed us warmly.

I took the train back to Malmo, Sweden, to be with my cousin Halinka for a few days and from there traveled to Stockholm to make another Danzig connection. I visited my former school friend Janka Krakowska Waril and her husband, Manu, both from my hometown. After a week with them I returned to New York.

I had too many impressions, too many details to share with my son, Benno, and his wife, Joy, in a short visit. I had to put it on paper. When Benno read my diary, he decided to make this journey too. He wanted to share this part of my life. By now he and Joy were parents of two children. Melanie was two and a half when her brother, Michael Max, was born. My grandson arrived almost nine months after Max died, so he was named for his grandfather and for my father: Mordchai Moshe in Hebrew.

Benno, an attorney, does nothing without deliberation and preparation. To go to Poland he wanted to be able to speak the language. Both of my sons understood every word but were not fluent in speaking. Two years later Benno was ready to go. He had learned to read, write, and speak (some) Polish. So in May 1993 he and I went to Poland. This trip was different. Benno did not need a translator. When Jozio met us at the new and modern Warsaw airport, we all spoke Polish. I saw a distraught Jozio. His wife Krysia was ill, and his son, Czarek, was separated from his wife. But he was happy to see us, to meet my oldest son, and most of all to be able to speak directly to him. As he did the previous time, he gave us a week of his time to help us see what I wanted Benno to see. We retraced the trip to Piotrkow, to Tomaszow, to Danzig, Zoppot, Orlowo, and Gdynia. On the way back to Warsaw, we stopped in the city of Kalisz, my mother's birthplace. Kalisz had the oldest Jewish community, the oldest Jewish cemetery, because in 1264 the Polish king, Boleslaw the Pious, granted Jews special privilege in "the Kalisz Statutes." My brother and I had come to this city each spring to celebrate the Passover holidays with both sets of grandparents. I took Benno to the streets where both my paternal and maternal grandparents once lived. My maternal grandparents' house had been destroyed during the war. My son and I retraced the steps my brother and I had taken so many times.

From Kalisz we drove one hour to the city of Lodz, where my Aunt Rose and her family once lived. The street and house looked older, neglected. The whole city was a depressing sight. We went to the house where my paternal grandparents lived in 1938. Only memories remained, but I could still see the faces of my family that was no more.

On the way back to Warsaw, Benno asked Jozio to stop again in Piotrkow, only fifty kilometers from Lodz. He wanted to visit the Jewish cemetery that I described in my diary. We found a Polish caretaker living next to the cemetery, and we asked if she could help us find Max's parents' graves. While she leafed through her notebook, I saw the name Kimmelman Malka, died April 1925—Max's mother. But we did not find Max's father's grave. The caretaker took us to his mother's grave site, which was only a few steps away from the monument in memory of the Bund fighters. Here Benno stood before the monument to honor the uncle he never knew, to pay tribute to the uncle whose name he bears. The most emotional moment for me was standing in front of Max's mother's grave. He adored and felt so proud of his mother. Being the last of her ten children, he had lost her when he was only seventeen. For many years Max had told me how much he would like to be at his mother's grave. Now we were fulfilling his wish. His son stood at the grave of his grandmother, after whom his daughter, Melanie, is named. In silence we stood at the stone that bore the name of Malka Kimmelman, beloved wife of Itzchak Kimmelman. I shall never forget this moment, and neither will Benno. The stone was tilted forward, the writing hard to read. We spoke with the caretaker, whose son was refinishing and repairing gravestones. We left Jozio money to pay the caretaker for repair of Max's mother's stone. Perhaps one day Benno will return here with his children and share with them what I have shared with him.

Back in Warsaw, we told Krysia about our discovery in Piotrkow. Then for the last part of this memorable journey we left for Treblinka. Benno had to see and experience what I saw in 1990. I was only sorry that Gene and Caroline did not have a chance to go there. What a harrowing experience to see the vastness and absolute stillness of Treblinka. For Benno it left an unforgettable impression. As we wandered amidst the broken stones, reading names of the seventeen thousand destroyed Jewish communities, the immense destruction of Jewish lives in Europe became a reality. Treblinka has to be seen and felt. It is impossible to describe.

So I had three journeys into the past, each one different. For Max as well as for me I returned. For the sake of my children and their children I bared my soul. For the sake of all family members we recalled the memories of those taken from us so brutally.

# EPILOGUE

During the most difficult times of World War II, I wondered whether the world really knew what was happening to us. I lived in total isolation, not knowing what was taking place outside the ghetto gates, outside the barbed wires of concentration camps. After the war, would anyone ever believe my experiences?

Not able to write things down while in camp, I trained myself to remember; to memorize most of the events I experienced. Almost thirty-five years later I sat down to write about them for the first time. Two things motivated me. First, I heard someone say that, if things are not written down, they never really happened. Second, my visit to the Jewish Museum in New York City and to Emory University in Atlanta, where Jewish artifacts from Danzig were exhibited, motivated me to put my memories on paper.

The exhibition showed religious objects and ceremonial articles from the Danzig synagogues. One part of the exhibit was from the Mattenbuden, the oldest synagogue in Danzig. My parents and I had attended this house of worship, and seeing the exhibit triggered strong recollections of my childhood. Today this city belongs to Poland and is called Gdansk, yet I think of it by the name I knew for so long.

As a Free City, Danzig attracted many refugees from Russia as they fled the revolution, including Jewish scholars from Lithuania, Poland, and Hungary. These so-called "Ostjuden," or Eastern Jews, enriched the Jewish community of Danzig with their talents, scholarship, art, and trade. Many of my parents' friends came to Danzig from the East. We were friends with Jews from the East as well as Jews from Germany, Prussia, and Austria. All of us suffered the same fate. The few surviving Danzig Jews now live all over the world, but their love of Danzig is a strong bond.

This book was written in memory of all my loved ones, members of my family who perished as well as friends who met their deaths during World War II. The dead cannot speak; they cannot be witnesses to the unspeakable horrors. I am their witness, and my years are numbered. I have to do it for them.

The new generation learns about the Holocaust through what is written and from those of us left. For some, I am the first Jewish person they have met. For most I am their first contact with a Holocaust survivor. After they listen to me, I ask for one and only one thing: *Remember* what I've told you. The burden of remembering is now with them. Once the voices of the survivors are stilled forever, the listeners will bear the burden of our memories. They must transmit what we've told them to their children and grandchildren. If only 1 or 2 percent of the people I have spoken to carry on the truth of the Holocaust, I will be satisfied. But will they do it? Or will the voices of those who claim the Holocaust never happened prevail? Agonizing as it is each time I speak, I know how important it is.

Hearing and seeing only numbers, listeners and readers have a hard time grasping the immensity of what happened, or feeling it personally. Six million Jews perished. Of those, one and a half million were children. But these are mere numbers; the impact is greater when there is a name and a face they can identify with.

During the past decade, people who deny that the Holocaust ever happened have sprung up like mushrooms after the rain. Their voices are heard

Mira's cousin, Jasio Hammer, age two.
The son of Henry and Rosa Hammer, he
and his mother were killed at Treblinka
when Jasio was eight.

Mira's mother, Genia Ryczke, with Mira's
Aunt Rosa Hammer in Kalisz, Poland, in
1934. Both were killed at Treblinka in
1942.

Mira's Aunt Rose Ryczke Przedecka with daughter, Gina, and husband, Marcus, in Krynica, Poland, in 1938. All were killed during the Holocaust.

Mira's cousin, Michael Lachman, with his and Mira's Uncle Henry Hammer in Vineland, N.J., 1967. Michael lives in Israel. Uncle Henry died in 1989.

Mira's family in 1993. From left, Gene, Caroline, Mira, Joy, and Benno.

Benno and Joy's children, Mira's grandchildren: Michael Max and Melanie. 1993.

everywhere, in almost every country. To argue with them is futile. They claim to have "proof." Fortunately for us and for history, Hitler's henchmen took pictures of atrocities, and German efficiency preserved them. Pictures from German archives taken during the war are available. Pictures taken by liberating armies are also *proof.*

Most of all we have the names of our dear ones who were taken away, torn from their families and never seen again. Here are the names and ages of family members who were Holocaust victims and places where they perished.

> My mother—Genia Hammer Ryczke, age 45; killed at Treblinka
> Paternal grandparents—Esther and Ephraim Ryczke, 75; Treblinka
> Aunt Gustava Hammer Lachman, age 47; husband David; Treblinka
> Cousin Marysia Lachman, 21; son, age 2; husband, 22; Treblinka
> Aunt Helen Hammer Krzewin, 42; husband, Zygmunt Krzewin, 44;
>     Treblinka
> Aunt Rosa Kaplan Hammer, 35; son, Joseph, 8; Treblinka
> Uncle Marcus Przedecki, 48; Treblinka
> Aunt Rose Ryczke Przedecka, 47; daughters, Halina, 26, and Gina, 22;
>     killed in Warsaw
> Maternal grandparents, Sarah and Shlomo Hammer, 73; Warsaw
> Uncle Heinrich Ryczke, 37; killed in Plaszow
> Brother Benno Ryczke, 17; killed at Mauthausen

Twenty members of my immediate family: all of them killed. Young and old, women, men, and children. Only my father and I survived the camps. Three more members of my family emerged from hiding or from surviving in Russia. My mother's brother, Henry Hammer, was harbored by Polish Catholic friends. He lost his wife and only son. My cousin Michael Lachman, who lost his parents, sister, baby-nephew, and brother-in-law, survived in Russia. My youngest cousin, Gustaw Krzewin (Tony Gorbutt, his Aryan name), escaped to Germany with the help of Polish non-Jewish friends but lost his parents. Today only my cousin Michael Lachman and I are alive.

In spite of all the evil and cruel experiences, I also saw the goodness of people. Friends and relatives were saved by Poles, Germans, French, and Dutch. Some of the rescuers were uneducated peasants, some were educated people, but all listened to their hearts even when they put themselves in danger. They risked their lives to save Jews from a certain death. These selfless and courageous people, regardless of nationality or religion, were the unsung heroes of the Holocaust years.

The tragic facts cannot be denied. This memoir has been written amidst many tears, sleepless nights, and agonizing moments. It is a memorial to those who were killed. My children and their children will become the guardians of these memories. If future generations fail to protect the truth, it vanishes. By keeping memories alive, by fighting those who deny the Holocaust, we fulfill the duty to *remember.*

The Holocaust is a lesson in human (and inhumane) history that took place because of hate, bigotry, indifference—all characteristics that know no bounds. These traits spread like wildfire. If we remain indifferent to human suffering, it can happen again; it can happen here, and who knows who the next victims will be? Only by remembering the bitter lesson of Hitler's legacy can we hope it will never be repeated. Teach it, tell it, read it.

# INDEX